THE VALUATION OF HUMAN LIFE

THE VALUATION OF HUMAN LIFE

GAVIN H. MOONEY, M.A.

Department of Community Medicine, University of Aberdeen, Scotland

First published 1977 by
THE MACMILLAN PRESS LTD
London and Basingstoke
Associated companies in Delhi Dublin Hong Kong Johannesburg
Lagos Melbourne New York Singapore and Tokyo

ISBN 0 333 21422 6

Printed in Great Britain at The Spottiswoode Ballantyne Press
by William Clowes and Sons Limited,
London, Colchester and Beccles

To the memory of my mother

Contents

Preface

Several thousand million pounds are devoted each year in Britain, as in other countries, to extending life and reducing disability, sickness and disease. Such expenditure is handled by many different agencies—such as ordinary citizens, private firms, local authorities, government departments. The interest of this book is restricted to decision-making in the public sector which relates to life saving, increasing life expectation or, as it is perhaps best defined, reducing the risk of death.

Decisions have to be reached within the public sector on how to deploy resources to the various apparently ever-increasing demands of different policy areas. Education, health, housing and many other worthy public sector activities could, if permitted, consume much more by way of resources than any government could foreseeably raise from the tax-payer. And as expenditure has to be constrained in the public sector, so public sector decision-makers have to choose what services to give what priority.

But the 'output' of the public sector is frequently difficult to measure and more frequently still difficult to evaluate. This is nowhere more so than in such policy areas as health care and road safety where part of the output is to be measured in terms of lives saved or reduced mortality. Yet once we accept that resources available for the health service are not infinite, this immediately implies that we must set some limit to the amount of resources which society can devote to saving life.

This book comprises an attempt to examine how we might set about answering the question: how much is society prepared to pay to reduce mortality; or more brutally, *what is the value of human life*? The justification for attempting to answer such questions lies in the desirability of injecting increased explicitness and rationality into decision-making in those areas of the public sector which are concerned with life saving. Given that resources are already being deployed to such activities as crash-barriers on motorways, helicopters for air–sea rescue, kidney machines and other life-saving measures—although such activities result only in a reduction in risk of death, not its elimination, in the policy fields affected—this means that already at the present time, at least by implication, values are being placed by decision-makers on the saving of life.

In 1970 when I first became involved in the issue of life valuation when working as an Economic Assistant in the Road Safety Directorate of the Ministry of Transport, it was a very 'unfashionable' area in which to be involved. The last few years have seen a quite remarkable growth in the area both in terms of the number of people interested and the 'intellectual respectability' of the subject matter. If this book can in any way further this growth or assist in improving the quality of decision-making in those public sector policy areas which are involved with life saving, then I will be well satisfied.

The book is directed at a somewhat disparate readership. It is written at such a level as not to be insulting to fellow economists, whereas at the same time it should not be too daunting or technical for public sector administrators—particularly those in health care and road safety; and, it is also hoped, that it will be sufficiently interesting to appeal to the educated lay person.

Many people have contributed in different ways to this book. In particular I would wish to thank Archie Cochrane for his assistance and the Abbotshill Trust for their financial support.

My thanks are also due to Tony Harrison who kept jogging my arm for six years to produce something in this field and who gave valuable criticism and advice at various stages of the compilation. I am also indebted for comments to Ianthe Fordyce, John Hutton, Alan Lassiere, Colin Mowl, David Pole, Elizabeth Russell, Ian Stevenson, Marolyn Young and many others. Parts of the manuscript have also benefited from discussion at seminars in the Civil Service and the Department of Political Economy in Aberdeen, and my thanks are due to my past and present colleagues for their comments.

To Shirley Bruscini, Lily Robertson and Isabel Tudhope for their enthusiastic help in the typing and retyping of scruffy manuscripts, I am most grateful.

Any errors which remain are of course my sole responsibility. The views expressed are mine and do not necessarily coincide with those of either the Department of Transport or the Department of Health and Social Security.

Aberdeen, 1977   G.H.M.

1

What is the Problem?

1.1 EXAMPLES IN LIFE-SAVING DECISION-MAKING

1.1.1 *Accidents Involving Broken-down Vehicles*

The presence of broken-down vehicles at the roadside creates a potential hazard for road users. Two possible ways of reducing it are first to require vehicles to be fitted with four-way flashers (which means that all four indicators flash together) or second to require that all drivers carry hazard warning triangles which in the event of a breakdown must be placed some distance behind the vehicle to warn other drivers of the hazard. The nature of the effects of these measures is similar, in other words, to a reduction in the number of accidents involving broken-down vehicles. A comparison of the costs and effectiveness (in terms of the reduction in hazard accidents achieved) will allow statements to be made to the effect that the cost per accident prevented is £x and £y respectively for the two methods. The choice between the two methods can then be made simply in terms of the less-expensive method per accident prevented. Note that in this case the objectives involved are identical, namely the reduction of these hazard accidents.

Even in this simple example however, problems arise with the use of this technique of 'cost-effectiveness' as a decision-aiding tool. While the technique does allow at least an ordinal ranking of the measures being considered, difficulties can arise over the question of whether the best choice in cost-effectiveness terms should be implemented. We might find that x and y above were 10 and 20 in which case there is little doubt that action would be implemented. If the figures were 10 000 and 20 000 some doubt as to the wisdom of the action would almost certainly arise and if they were 10 million and 20 million then both measures would be ruled out. Thus cost-effectiveness on its own

1

can reduce many areas of uncertainty for the decision-maker but leaves large areas untouched. As a technique it is concerned more with the mechanics of policy than the strategy.

To complicate the issue further and extend the point just made, let us assume that the four-way flasher system would cost £5 million per annum and save 5000 hazard accidents at a cost per accident saved of £1000. The hazard warning triangle on the other hand would cost annually (say) £7.5 million and save 6000 hazard accidents at a cost per accident saved of £1250. On the straightforward basis of decision-making outlined above the four-way flasher system would be preferred. But faced with these calculations what decision would the decision-maker reach? Might he not argue that the extra £2.5 million for an additional saving of 1000 hazard accidents at an additional cost of £2500 each was justified? After all the average cost per accident saved would only be increased from £1000 to £1250. The point here is that with this cost-effectiveness analysis no guidance is given as to whether measures should be implemented at all even although it is possible to produce some ranking of the measures to meet a specific objective.

A further complication can be written into this same example by introducing the other possible solution to the problem, namely the provision of a hard shoulder or of laybys. Such provision however gives rise to other benefits. For example the availability of laybys will make stopping at the roadside for reasons other than breakdown possible without any reduction in the capacity of the road. It is difficult to deal with these additional benefits in cost-effectiveness analyses.

But the choice faced may be still more complicated. In choosing between improving the sightlines at a junction, requiring that the depth of tyre treads be a minimum of x millimetres and a measure to prevent hazard accidents, cost-effectiveness techniques begin to break down. It is possible to state the objective simply in terms of accidents saved as before, but the nature of the accidents at junctions may be quite different from those resulting from bald treads; the average numbers of casualties per accident may vary according to the type of accident, or the amount of damage per accident may differ, etc. Consequently, to express all these measures in terms of the same objective of simply reducing accidents begins to look rather crude. The issue is complicated still further if we wish to compare the above measures with certain secondary measures such as the fitting of head restraints to the front seats of cars. These will have no effect on the number of accidents but simply reduce the number or severity of casualties. A ranking of priorities in terms of the cost per accident prevented is obviously a nonsense in this last case. Of course cost per accident prevented is not the only base for cost-effectiveness in road safety; other measures which have been used include cost per casualty saved, per death prevented and per fatal accident prevented. None of these is in practice much of an improvement if any. Using a casualty base means that no account is taken of damage costs and none of differing severities of casualties.

1.1.2 *Renal Failure*

In the evaluation of health care, the limitations of the usefulness of cost-effectiveness analysis can again be indicated. Studies have been made of the cost-effectiveness of treatment for renal failure, a disease which will normally kill. Some sufferers can be kept alive through dialysis or by transplant. One such study by Klarman *et al.*[1] has compared the costs of dialysis and the costs of transplantation against the years of life which each saves. Dialysis can be a rather horrific process for the patient and may lead to psychiatric problems both in the patient himself and his close family. Consequently Klarman's study 'allowed' for the lower quality of life of the dialysis patients by suggesting that a year of life extension on dialysis was only equivalent to three-quarters of a year's extension on transplantation. Assuming, having made this adjustment, that thereafter a year of life is a year of life whenever and to whomever it falls it was then possible to show that per unit of expenditure transplantation was a better buy than dialysis. What the study did not—nor could it—show was whether transplantation itself was worthwhile either in some absolute sense or in terms of the opportunity cost involved in spending less on varicose veins treatment, research on the common cold or whatever.

1.1.3 *Deficiencies of Cost-effectiveness Analysis*

Thus the problems of cost-effectiveness stem firstly from the fact that it does not allow for the possibility of more than one type of benefit and secondly does not permit anything to be said about the absolute, as opposed to the relative, value of the measure in question. This latter point when extended to any life-saving area of policy means that cost-effectiveness cannot tell us what the overall budgets in such areas ought to be. (This may not be a major drawback in that to a considerable extent the decision on this question will be a political one anyway. Nonetheless if economic techniques can be brought to bear on this question of the appropriate size of budgets in such areas as health care and safety it may have an effect on the political decision as to what the size should be.) Cost-effectiveness analysis is thus a useful tool in determining what techniques to use to obtain some objective; it is of little help in determining what relative priorities to set on differing and competing objectives.

The deficiencies in cost-effectiveness analysis point to the desirability of adopting an analytical methodology which allows all the effects to be measured in a common currency and which permits different sub-objectives to be considered together. Cost-benefit analysis (C.B.A.) can provide the necessary framework. The principal difference between the two is that in cost-benefit analysis monetary values are placed on the effects of the different measures. Once a system is introduced which places the saving of life, reduction in damage etc., on the same measuring rod (of money) then making the necessary additions or trade-offs between the different outputs from life-saving measures is a relatively simple matter.

Cost-benefit analysis at the same time permits, in theory at least, a decision to be made as to the optimal level of allocation of resources to life-saving areas. By placing values on the different outputs it not only allows a ranking in order of priority of projects but also indicates the point at which the costs of a measure exceed the benefits. It is at the point where marginal costs equal marginal benefits that the optimum budget lies. At this stage therefore it is sufficient to say that the basic reason for arguing that we need to value human life is to make use of the virtues of cost-benefit analysis in place of the simpler and cruder cost-effectiveness techniques. A fuller description of C.B.A. is presented in chapter 2.

1.2   A JUSTIFICATION FOR TACKLING THE PROBLEM

The above examples serve to highlight the nature of the problems of decision-making in life-saving policy areas but even so the valuation of human life may appear to some an immoral task. To some potential readers the fact than an economist should even contemplate such a task may simply serve as further evidence with which to confirm certain scarcely contained feelings that the economic profession likes to see itself as playing God. Without looking to the field of macroeconomics—where economists may well have appeared to wish to play God but in many eyes have been shown to be very much second-rate prophets—the evidence of this from the past includes such pastimes as placing monetary values on ancient monuments, measuring the cost of airport noise, valuing leisure time and putting price-tags on countless other 'priceless' articles. The title of this book may well provide the final nail in the coffin as far as some readers' views on economists and economics are concerned. For others perhaps they will get beyond a reading of this introductory chapter and seek to obtain an insight into a valuation problem that has been with us (although not explicitly) since the beginning of mankind.

Whatever the motivation—an awareness that there is much to be said for making the value of life explicit, a straightforward curiosity, an interest in decision-making in life-saving activities, a morbid satisfaction in reading about death or whatever—it is as well to put the record straight at this juncture and make it clear that at no point in this book is it possible to find a numerical sum which can be claimed to be '*the* value of human life'. It is doubtful if such a thing could exist in terms, that is, of there being a single value.* Given that there is not, in the normally accepted use of the word, a 'market' for life, we cannot simply look to the market price of the product life to determine what monetary value to place on it, as we might do in the case of peas, cars or toothpaste. This problem of evaluating products not normally having a price-tag attached to them is of course not peculiar to valuation of life. For example, in attempting to estimate the value of a new road, we require to know how the users value the time-savings they will obtain from the road. If in our valuation methods we were only concerned to look at goods and services which were included in Gross National Product (G.N.P.) then we could safely ignore such matters as leisure-time savings. However to use a G.N.P.-based value system would be to ignore the fact that individuals are prepared to pay for certain 'goods' which are not included in G.N.P. Such goods include reduction in traffic noise, preservation of the seashore, a cleaner atmosphere, etc. All we require to establish that something has positive value for which a monetary valuation could exist is that

---

* But see appendix C for some values emerging from various different approaches.

individuals in society would be prepared to pay some positive monetary sum for that 'something'. Or expressed differently we might say that were for example clean air available in the market place then there would be a demand for such a product. The same applies to the product of reduced risk of death.

At present within many parts of the public sector—health care, road safety, fire prevention, etc.—resource allocation decisions are made on what to spend (and what not to spend) on various projects which might influence the level of mortality risk which individuals face, that is, on how much to spend on saving life. What we examine in this book are the various methods which are available for trying to estimate what values should be placed on such life-saving activities and the advantages and disadvantages of the various approaches.

One of the main reasons for tackling this problem is that there exists some evidence, which we will discuss in more detail in chapter 6, that there are major inconsistencies in current decision-making in the field of saving of life. Such inconsistencies suggest that life is much more highly valued in some fields than others. While we can postulate certain arguments to defend some differentials between life values (for example, differing life expectation of the lives at risk) the differentials appear so great as to suggest some misallocation of resources within life-saving activities. By moving towards a more explicit valuation process one advantage could be to reduce these inconsistencies and thereby provide an increase in the total benefit of investments in life saving. As Harrison[2] has written: 'The desire to be consistent, to ensure that the values attached in one sphere for a given effect or output ... of public policy are similar to those attached to it elsewhere, no matter which area of government is responsible for the relevant policy, may serve to make the public sector decision process more rational, in ways which all would accept'.

1.3 WHAT DO WE WANT TO MEASURE?

1.3.1 *The Individual and Risk of Death*

Our starting point in seeking a methodology for valuation in the field of life saving is that frequently within the framework of our governmental institutions it is considered that the views and preferences of the members of society ought to be the basis of the valuation methodology used in public decision-making. This is of course a value judgment but it is one which would probably be accepted by most members of our parliamentary democracy. While the underlying political philosophy here is of sbme interest and the nature of the freedoms and constraints of our political system worthy of detailed discussion, further consideration of these issues is delayed until chapter 2. For the present it will be assumed that the reader will either accept the basic tenet or at the least delay judgment until that later discussion. There are of course areas where the only real sanction on government is in the end the ballot box. Even then this may not be a very real constraint if in what is essentially a two-party system there are considerable areas of agreement between the parties, as it might well be argued is the case in Britain today. None the less even in such areas as these there is likely to be an attempt to at least reflect the wishes and desires of the society in so far as these are known or are knowable. (It is frequently in interpretation that the real difficulty lies.) It is against this assessment of the relationship between the wishes of the electorate and the actions of the democratically elected government that we now search for our methodology. What has been said about political philosophy here is no more than setting the political framework within which cost-benefit analysis would have free rein.

Against this background we must go on to consider what it is that we want to measure—and to try to see this from the standpoint of the individuals in society. Taking the example of road safety, while it is true that each year in Britain there are about 7000 to 8000 deaths in road accidents, from the point of view of the individual road user these figures are almost meaningless. The victims are anonymous up until the time they are killed. We do know that certain groups are more at risk than others—the young and the old pedestrian as opposed to the middle-aged, the teenage car driver, etc. We have no way of identifying just who the individual victims will be. In health care the situation at first sight might appear rather different in that there will be occasions where a doctor can identify individuals who will die on a particular day or who would die but for the intervention of some form of medical treatment. However, it is not this particular decision environment with which we are here concerned. In so far as economics is used within the field of health care then the type of decisions with which it is concerned are much more global than the question of intervention at a time when the actual individuals at risk are immediately identifiable. In the economics of health care what is involved is more the question of the allocation of resources in terms of which groups within the community ought to receive more; where can scarce resources be most effectively used in reducing the loss of welfare associated with different diseases or conditions; can some substitution of certain factors of production of health for certain other factors—home care for hospital care; ancillary workers for highly trained nurses—result in some scarce resources being more productively used. In so far as individuals at risk are relevant in deciding upon such questions as these, our interest is very much at the level of considering the risks facing society as a whole or facing certain groups within society, for example the risk of men over 50 dying from lung cancer; or the differential mortality risk of a newborn child at different weights. These kinds of risk are, as can immediately be seen, very similar to those just considered for the road safety case.

In some instances the individual will be broadly aware of the fact that he or she faces some risk of death—the motorist travelling from London to Birmingham will know that there is some chance that he won't make it alive; the individual, and naturally more so the elderly person, in planning the coming summer's holiday will be cognisant of the fact that he may not be alive to go on holiday. This risk of death will not always be something which is considered at a conscious level and frequently even when it is as individuals we would have little idea as to what the relevant level of risk is.

Consider our London to Birmingham motorist. Were he to consider the risk involved in his journey then as well as allowing for the other costs involved in the trip he would also consider the 'cost' of the risk. It is possible that such an individual might decide that having weighed up all the costs including the risk and the benefits of making the trip he will go ahead and make the journey by car as planned. In so far as he does rationalise his decision then he is simply arguing that taking all things into account including the risk involved the benefits of the trip are greater than the costs. He thus accepts the risk involved. However, he might decide that taking all the costs into account, the benefits do not appear sufficiently great to make the car journey. In this case he has two possible options open to him. Firstly if he can reduce his costs in some way then the journey may still be capable of yielding positive net benefits to him. For example, we could assume that the costs of travelling by train were as for by car with the exception of risk which was smaller for the train. Then if it only required a relatively small reduction in total cost to persuade our individual to go to Birmingham this reduction in risk might be sufficient. Secondly, our individual might decide that—assuming other costs fixed and benefits fixed —there is no way in which he can reduce his risk or reduce it sufficiently to make it worth his while to make the trip.

In attempting to model how a rational man *might* consider the problem then the above description does not seem unreasonable. What is suggested is that when individuals *do* get round to considering the problem of death then it is very much in this 'risk/cost/benefit' context in which they will view it. It follows from this that in attempting to place a 'value on life' we are seeking a methodology in tune with the individual's view of death, a methodology which allows individuals to value reductions in risk of death. Thus what we want to try to measure—initially at least—is how much an individual would be prepared to pay to reduce his risk of dying from x to $x - y$ where x and y are small. In adopting this particular stand on the relevance of the individual both as regards how he views the question of life and death and the value he places upon changes in the level of risk of death we are in effect accepting the basic premise as spelt out by Jones-Lee[3]

'If cost-benefit analysis is to be employed *and* the consumer's surplus approach adopted for those goods for which market information *is* available then consistency would seem to demand the development of procedures for eliciting some indication of the sums individuals would be prepared to forfeit to effect changes in the level of provision of those goods for which market information is not available'.

It is therefore a central assumption of any methodology we wish to adopt, firstly that it attempts to reflect the views of those whose lives are likely to be at risk and secondly that the problem is posed in such a way that potential victims can recognise the type of situation which they themselves see.

Having said this, we must recognise that the conditions required to implement this ideal may not obtain. For example, it may be that we cannot devise a method to obtain the values we seek in this ideal approach and we may then have to settle for some alternative methodology. Or again it may be that individuals wish themselves to be subject to greater paternalism than is implied by this method. Yet again, given the inevitably political nature of the decision on what values to use, we must accept that whatever approach may appear 'ideal' in our thinking may not be to the relevant political decision-makers. However, as Harrison[2] (page 20) indicates: 'The individual and social valuation must necessarily diverge, but this does not negate the basic principle; rather it suggests enlarging the number of individuals considered in any particular case'.

In recognising that our ideal may not be obtainable, it then becomes necessary to judge the effect of making allowance for various contraints. We will therefore discuss a number of approaches to life valuation as well as our preferred methodology, indicating their various merits and disadvantages and how the existence of different constraints might lead us to accept one or other of these approaches. In addition we will discuss in some detail just how far it appears reasonable to accept the primacy of the individual and the extent to which we can embrace the concept of 'consumer sovereignty'.

But returning to our suggested ideal, what we would wish to propose is that the benefits of any project which reduces mortality should be assessed in terms of what individuals would be prepared to pay to obtain this reduction. For example, in the case of road safety, Harrison[2] (page 14) has argued that 'the safety benefits to be attributed to a project should be defined as the sum of what individuals would be prepared to pay to reduce the risk of death or injury by the amount the project concerned is likely to influence it'. Thus the 'value of life' which would be relevant to a project which resulted in a reduction in risk of death of 0.001 for 1000 people would be the sum that those exposed to the risk plus their relatives, friends, etc.—indeed anyone who wished to contribute—would be prepared to pay to obtain this reduction.

1.3.2 *The Nature of Risk and Probability*

The idea of 'the risk of death' embodies a view of risk or probability which needs to be examined. The notion of probability can take different forms, two of which are of potential relevance here. Firstly there is the classical or frequency notion of probability which is most commonly exemplified by dice-throwing or coin-tossing. If an unbiased coin is tossed it is just as likely that it comes down heads as tails. Thus the probability of getting a head is a half. This type of probability refers to a situation where there is a finite number of well-defined possible outcomes, many repeated trials (which are independent of each other, in terms of outcome) and the emergence of stable frequencies for certain outcomes, as trials multiply.

Secondly, there is risk or probability which is based on the assessment of individuals, perhaps using some but not complete knowledge of the frequency type of probability above. We all form judgments about such probabilities, for example the probability that Manchester United will win the league, the risk of rain today, and so on. But clearly these judgments are based not on anything as 'objective' as frequencies of independent events but rather estimates by the individuals using what knowledge and experience they have available, in other words 'subjective' assessments.

In considering risk we draw a distinction between 'objective' risks and 'subjective' risks. While there are few if any situations in road safety or health which can be equated with the classical probability concept in its entirety, we have categorised the quasi-classical probability backed by 'expert' judgment as 'objective risk'. 'Subjective' risk is where the estimation is left to the subjective judgment of the individuals at risk. Thus while the definition of risk is not as clearcut in the case of road accidents as in coin-tossing, none the less we can make an 'objective' assessment of the probability of an average road user being killed on the roads with a high degree of accuracy. From previous years' data we know the numbers killed and trends therein. In combination with information about the population at risk we can then make an 'objective' estimate of the actual risk of death for the average road user.

Any individual can use the second notion of probability to assess his or her risk of dying from, say, lung cancer. This 'subjective' measurement of risk will have built into it various judgments, prejudices and bits of relevant and even irrelevant information. Indeed some of this information may relate to the individual's knowledge of the 'objective' risk of lung cancer.

The important aspects of this discussion of 'objective' and 'subjective' measurement of risk are that firstly the level of risk in the same situation may differ depending on which form of measure is used and secondly in policy-making we may be forced to choose between them. This can lead to difficulties. For example if a particular group of individuals believe that their risk of dying from cancer is 1 in 100 (that is, the subjective risk) when the 'objective' risk is only 1 in 1000, what risk factor should be used in any policy considerations of treating these patients? This distinction is of major concern to us in our deliberations and we will return to it in later chapters.

11

1.3.3. *Acceptability of the Methodolgy*

One other theme that is in many ways just as important to the applied economist is that any methodology devised must be seen to be logically founded by those administrators and decision-makers who are to be asked to use it. It is relatively easy to see that one of the major reasons why cost-benefit analysis has not been as widely used or accepted in decision-making in the health services as it has in other areas (such as transport) is that whereas the decision-makers in transport have come to accept the rationale behind the valuation of operating costs, time-savings, etc. (with some reservations of course) their opposite numbers in health have (quite rightly) been slow to accept the rationale behind valuing a man's life in terms of his economic output—which has been the method used to date (see chapter 5). There are other very sound reasons why cost-benefit analysis has been slow to make inroads into health care decision-making but the lack of a methodology which can be seen to be logical and well founded by the relevant decision-makers is a fundamental prerequisite to making advances in the use of cost-benefit analysis in any area of public decision-making.

1.4 THE NATURE OF THE TASK

This opening chapter has attempted to set the scene for the rest of the book. Some examples have been presented of the way in which the existence of values of life might assist decision-makers and a start has been made in indicating what it is we want to measure and the context in which this task is set.

In chapter 2 the nature of cost-benefit analysis and its relevance are outlined together with a statement of the philosophical basis on which the study rests. Chapters 3 and 4 describe in some detail decision-making in two policy areas where the saving of life is a major objective—road safety and health care.

Thereafter chapters 5 and 6 outline various approaches to valuation of life before in chapters 7 and 8 we examine what we have called the 'preferred valuation methodology'. Finally in chapter 9 the detailed rules for decision-making as indicated by the discussions in the other chapters are outlined.

In the appendixes the reader will find some comments on attitudes to death (appendix A), an outline of discounting procedures (appendix B) and some 'values of life' (appendix C).

REFERENCES

1. Klarman, H. E., Francis, J. O'S., and Rosenthal, G. D., Cost effectiveness analysis applied to the treatment of chronic disease, *Med. Care*, **6**, 48 (1968)
2. Harrison, A. J., *The Economics of Transport Appraisal*, Croom Helm, London, 14, 15 and 20 (1974)
3. Jones-Lee, M. W., Valuation of reduction in probability of death by road accident, *J. Transport Econ. Policy*, pp. 14 and 20, Jan. (1969)

2

Cost-benefit Analysis and Valuation of Life

2.1 COST-BENEFIT ANALYSIS

2.1.1 *What is Cost-benefit Analysis?*

In the previous chapter some introductory comments were made about cost-benefit analysis (C.B.A.). There are now available several books and articles which will provide the interested reader with a detailed account of the theory and practice of C.B.A.[1-6]. However, since the valuation process described here is claimed to rest on cost-benefit analysis and some readers may not be familiar with the theory and concepts used, this chapter attempts to indicate briefly what C.B.A. is about and thereby set the framework for the rest of the book.

Cost-benefit analysis is essentially a decision-aiding or decision-making tool. Turvey[7] sums this up neatly when he writes: 'Cost-benefit analysis can be understood in two senses. In one it consists simply of the work necessary to present a decision-taker with the information which he requires in order to make a decision. In the other sense it goes further and includes the task of taking the decision'. For our purpose it is sufficient to see C.B.A. in the former sense, as a decision-*aiding* tool.

Cost-benefit analysis is about choice. In the field of public administration decisions have to be made regarding the allocation of resources to such diverse activities as the building of new motorways, the level of doctors' remuneration, the provision of nursery school places, grants to the Arts Council and so on. In the private sector the allocation of resources is determined by and large by market forces.

14

When these market forces either do not or cannot operate on publicly provided goods and services then resort has to be made to other means to determine how best to allocate scarce resources.

One way of achieving this is through the use of cost-benefit analysis. For example, there is undoubtedly a demand for road space; road space is not priced (or at least not directly). Yet if we are to establish whether or not it is in any sense 'worthwhile' to build more roads, we need to know what the benefits are of so doing and what value to place upon them. It is a reasonably straightforward business to state what the nature of the benefits will be—savings in operating costs, savings in time and savings in accidents. Operating costs are directly measurable since the various component parts are available in the market place and we can accept the price of the goods in question—petrol, tyres, oil etc.—as a measure of this value. We can probably agree that savings in working time can be valued at the appropriate wage rate.

Savings in leisure time and savings in accidents are less straightforward. We need to know how much individuals would be prepared to pay for these benefits or in other words what 'demand' there is for these 'products'. What cost-benefit analysis in effect attempts to do is to estimate what the demand for such goods is and through the imputation of prices allows us to estimate what the value is of providing such benefits as savings in leisure time and savings in accidents. Setting such benefits against the cost of providing them allows us to see whether the net benefit (benefits minus costs) is positive or negative. It is taken as given—a basic tenet of cost-benefit analysis—that something is only worth doing if the benefit of doing it exceeds the cost. (It should be noted that this is a necessary condition for something to be 'passed' by cost-benefit analysis. It may not be a sufficient condition.)

There are several difficulties which arise in the move from the concept of costs and revenues in the private sector to that of costs and benefits in the public sector. One of these is that it is frequently difficult or impossible either to measure or evaluate some of the benefits arising from a particular project. In the language of cost-benefit analysis these are normally referred to as the 'intangibles'. On intangibles Newton[8] writes: 'The whole question of "intangible" costs and benefits is one which has dominated the analytical development of cost-benefit analysis ... Most of the social costs and benefits of public projects were originally considered to be intangible. However, it is

15

important to note that what was considered to be an intangible yesterday may not be an intangible today'.

What we are trying to do is to make one of today's intangibles —saving of life or reducing mortality—no longer one of tomorrow's intangibles. To those sceptical that this might be done one might be permitted to quote Weisbrod[9]: 'In the Middle Ages and earlier, surely it must have been argued by some that one's feeling of warmth or cold was intangible, unmeasurable and so on. Fortunately Gabriel Fahrenheit did not agree . . .'.

It is easy to overstate the contribution which cost-benefit analysis can make to decision-making in the public sector. Many of the attacks which have been made on it have stemmed from a misunderstanding (for which professional economists are largely to blame) of what cost-benefit analysis could achieve and what its limitations are. Newton[8] writes: 'In summing up cost-benefit analysis, it is . . . important to emphasise that the technique is not viewed as a substitute for decision-making, nor as a panacea for the problem of resource allocation in the public sector. It does not simplify the task of management by unfailingly producing the "right" answer. Its claim to recognition lies in the truism that the quality of the decisions depends on the quality of available information upon which the decisions are based. Cost-benefit analysis assists decision-makers by giving them *better* (not necessarily *more*) information—what use is made of the information is not the direct concern of the analyst. In public affairs, the final decision will always be political, and may in part be intuitive. But it will be a better decision if it is preceded by as much quantification as possible'.

2.1.2 *The Concept of Consumer Sovereignty*

There is no need here to dwell on the more esoteric theoretical and conceptual problems associated with cost-benefit analysis. However, it is worth raising one specific issue—consumer sovereignty. Boldly stated the concept of consumer sovereignty suggests that the individual affected by any project being considered is the best judge of its value. Thus in cost-benefit analysis, when we are valuing benefits, in answering the question 'value to whom?' the answer wherever possible is 'value to the consumer'. This concept of consumer sovereignty is a basis tenet of cost-benefit analysis as it is normally conceived. Consequently it is incumbent upon the economist to try to avoid imposing *his* values or the politicians' values or the administrators' values on the benefits from a particular investment, but rather to attempt to determine what value the potential beneficiaries place on the benefits. At the same time it should be the value placed by any losers on any costs involved which determines the valuation of the costs.

Where intangibles today remain intangibles tomorrow then it may well be that the politicians will have to judge what values to place on them. Indeed if the politicians or whoever are the community leaders so wish they are of course free to *impose* their valuations on the benefits. But it is assumed that the norm of our democratic public decisions is to take account of and to reflect the electorate's preferences.

2.2 WHY SHOULD WE WANT TO VALUE LIFE?

Perhaps, however, we need to consider a more fundamental question than simply the advantages of being able to place a value on life. Why is it that we are even in a position to want to do so? What is it about the good that requires that we turn our minds to how to value it? Why is it that this good is not available in the market place in the way that peas, books and lawn mowers are?

A considerable body of literature—economic, political, social, etc.—exists which considers the role of government and of government expenditure in the economy. Certain roles are performed by the government which require the use of economic resources. Some of these—national defence, for example—could hardly be provided in any other way. Others, such as education can be provided both publicly and privately. Others again—regional industrial development, for example—involve a combination of public and private funds. In some instances the government does not intervene to the extent of becoming financially involved but legislates to protect individuals in various ways (the Trades Descriptions Act, for example). In yet other cases the government does not interfere in any way with the individual consumer's preferences.

Much of our difficulty in the area of life saving lies in the fact that several of these elements are present at one and the same time. Like national defence, road safety has in some respects the attributes of a 'public good'.* Like education, health care can be provided both

---

* The main attributes of a 'public good' are firstly that the benefit any individual obtains from it is a function of the total amount of the good available and secondly the consumption of a public good by one individual does not diminish the amount available for others. Other examples are public parks and lighthouses.

publicly and privately. Like regional development it could (although it could be argued it does not) prove possible to allocate public money to provide private incentives to greater safety (not through legislation but, for example, by charging differential premiums to employers for the financing of the Industrial Injuries Scheme). Through the Construction and Use Regulations the government lays down certain minimum requirements for vehicle design thereby giving protection to car users and purchasers. Certain aspects of safety are left wholly to the individual. (Although not required by law there are many safety features which individuals have fitted to their vehicles at least partly in the interests of increased safety such as head restraints, four-way flashers, etc.) Why the government is active in the field of reducing mortality stems from this diverse nature of life-saving policies. At the same time this provides an explanation of why we are in a position to want to value human life.

By accepting that the value of life is not infinite and that the benefits of saving lives have an opportunity cost in terms of school building, grants to the Arts Council, etc. we are rationalising what is already largely present in the decision-making processes. But in fact we go further. Just as we would argue in the case of the private firm that any costs external to the firm—washing dirtied from factory chimney smoke, lives lost and injuries sustained from dangerous machinery—should be internalised to the firm, so by and large this should be the case in the public sector as well. In assessing how far to go in preventing accidents, the policy of the firm ought to be to expand accident prevention measures up to the point at which marginal prevention costs equal the marginal accident-saving benefit. Similarly, for the government the policy to adopt is to maximise social welfare which in this context is to equate marginal social cost with marginal social benefit (in this instance in terms of lives saved). Note that this decision rule encompasses two important features

    (i) the value of life is not infinite;

    (ii) a value can be placed on the saving of life and equated with other factors also expressed in monetary units.

2.3   ATTITUDES TO RISK OF DEATH

Our attitudes to death and risk of death are complex phenomena. The way we react to risk through changes in our behaviour patterns as a result of our attitudes is consequently difficult to analyse. What can be said without fear of contradiction is that in the great majority of circumstances where life is threatened then most of us will react with some negative feeling, in other words the existence of the threat will result in some decrease in our welfare. Some risk situations will induce greater losses of utility than others. Situations where we perceive the threat to be greater for example will normally result in greater loss of welfare (although it may only be as a first approximation that we would assume that the disutility was in direct proportion to the level of risk as perceived). We might also argue that as the level of risk, measured in some objective manner, increases so our perceived level of risk will increase—but we are probably on shakier ground on this issue.

What is undoubtedly true however is that we do attempt to avoid risk frequently at some cost in terms of time or inconvenience. Most of the time we are largely unaware of these risks but the pattern of our behaviour is sometimes such that we obviously do make allowance for them. Sometimes we may be guided by others; sometimes we assess the same risk level differently from others and therefore act differently; and sometimes we act differently not because of a different assessment of the risk but because we feel better or less able to cope with the risk.

The way we as individuals deal with risk and our attitude to it are almost certainly functions of three different but associated variables. Firstly, there is the individual's assessment of the risk involved which will be influenced by his knowledge and experience. If we were to ask 100 individuals what the risk was of being killed on their flight from Heathrow to Turnhouse we would probably get 100 different answers.

Secondly, there is the individual's fear or anxiety associated with a given level of risk. Even if two individuals were agreed on the level of risk involved, one might fly and the other might not simply because of lesser and greater anxiety associated with the particular agreed level of risk. Thirdly, in many risk situations there are two factors present—the event which gives rise to the initial potential risk situation (such as an engine failure) and a probability of some preventive interception which will reduce the potential risk. Different individuals may have different perceptions of the influence or applicability of this latter type of factor. Thus attitudes to risk-taking and the ways in which we deal with it are a function of (a) our appraisal of the level of risk; (b) our anxiety level associated with this; (c) our appraisal of the remedial action available to eliminate or reduce the potential risk.

19

Now at the individual level (and assuming for the present that only the individuals directly involved in the risk are relevant) it can be argued that all these matters should be left to the individual. Indeed if an individual seeks positively to end his life (and he is, let us assume, a hermit) then it might be said that society ought not to interfere. Rightly or wrongly however society does interfere frequently; the individual who attempts to commit suicide is often saved by some 'do-gooder' dramatically saving him from the Thames. In our society it is deemed morally wrong (though since 1961 not legally wrong) to attempt to take one's own life. We adopt a paternalistic attitude to would-be suicides and do all within our powers as a society to prevent such events occurring. (Whether the sole motivation is to protect the individual concerned is another matter. For a fuller discussion of suicide see appendix A.)

On the issue of euthanasia and the right of society to take a life we as a society adopt a somewhat ambivalent attitude. While we are not prepared to go so far as to legalise euthanasia as such, at the same time we accept that the medical profession on occasion come close to practising it, admittedly in a passive form. Why we adopt such a posture is difficult to determine. One theory might be that the younger members of society tend to identify euthanasia not simply with the 'elderly', a rather anonymous body of people, but much more specifically with those whom—whether it be the case or not—they feel they ought to hold dear. In such circumstances we cannot bring ourselves to support a policy of euthanasia in that we see it personalised in a view explicitly associated with our own relationships with parents and grandparents. In so far as these individuals themselves wish euthanasia, we can never be certain as to why. Is it that they see themselves as a burden on us? Can *we* accept this without feelings of guilt? Despite the fact that they may wish their own lives to be ended we may not be able to bring ourselves to allow this, not out of any feelings for the person concerned but rather because of fear of our own guilt feelings. Lastly, we may also be concerned that euthanasia does not happen to *us* when we don't want it. Whatever the explanation there is little doubt that this is an area where rationalisation does not come easily.

2.4 THE PHILOSOPHICAL BASIS OF THE SOCIAL WELFARE FUNCTION

2.4.1 *Bentham and Mill*

Great emphasis is placed here on the concept of consumers' sovereignty and the desirability of taking account of consumers' preferences in determining the methodology for valuation of life and/or reduction in risk. Consequently in determining the nature of the social welfare function this view also prevails. (The expression 'social welfare' simply means benefit to society; thus the 'social welfare function' is the function which describes how the benefit to society is comprised in the relevant circumstances.) Embodied in this view is a fairly major expression of political and economic philosophy which accepts the economic calculus of Jeremy Bentham and the political philosophy of John Stuart Mill. What is suggested is that by placing a plus sign in front of all the benefits and a minus in front of all the costs and throwing them all in the same pot we can decide whether we have an improvement or not simply by examining the sign which emerges for the totality. This is commensurate with the utilitarian philosophy of the greatest happiness of the greatest number—provided that one important position is held. That is that in determining for each individual whether or not he or she *is* better off the individual is deemed the best judge for himself.

Mill has something of direct interest to say on this issue—at least in the special circumstances where the government goes so far as to compel individuals to protect themselves. He writes[10]: 'The proper object of sanitary laws is not to compel people to take care of their own health, but to prevent them from endangering the health of others. To prescribe by law, what they should do for their own health alone, would by most people be regarded as something like tyranny'.

Now admittedly in various fields of governmental activity (such as Mill's example of sanitation) at least part of the *raison d'etre* for government activity is to ensure that 'externalities' (effects on others) are not omitted from the economic calculus. To quote Mill[11] again: 'As soon as any part of a person's conduct affects prejudicially the interests of others, society has jurisdiction over it'.

We can accept Mill's defence of consumer sovereignty but it is a defence which appears to go too far. For it does not permit that situation where an individual may decide that it is in his own best

21

interest to allow the Government to use its better knowledge for his own good, or where the individual wishes the government to be paternalistic. Now we are here on very difficult ground and close to a position which might permit all sorts of authoritarian decisions to be made on the basis of the government acting for the betterment of man where man is not sufficiently well informed to see his own best interest.

2.4.2 *Liberty versus Coercion*

Berlin[12], in his classic essay on two concepts of liberty, writes: 'It is one thing to say that I know what is good for X, while he himself does not; and even to ignore his wishes for its—and his—sake; and a very different one to say that he has *eo ipso* chosen it, not indeed consciously, not as he seems in everyday life, but in his role as a rational self which his empirical self may not know—the "real" self which discerns the good, and cannot help choosing it once it is revealed'. Later Berlin continues: 'It is one thing to say that I may be coerced for my own good which I am too blind to see: this may, on occasion, be for my benefit; indeed it may enlarge the scope of my liberty; it is another to say that if it is my good then I am not being coerced, for I have willed it, whether I know this or not, and am free—or "truly" free—even while my poor earthly body and foolish mind bitterly rejects it, and struggle against those who seek however benevolently to impose it, with the greatest desperation'.

Berlin has here pushed us into a corner where it might appear that to advocate 'imposed' risk measurements (that is, the use of 'objective' risk functions) is in effect merely some sort of rather superficial 'cover-up' for what Berlin calls 'coercion'. There are in effect two issues here. Firstly there is no suggestion that we coerce people to do things against their wills—or at least not directly. The element of coercion which *may* be present is simply at the level of imposing various constraints on their degree of ignorance about the risk levels they face. By leaving individuals free to determine the *values* to be placed on benefits which befall them we are allowing them freedom to express their preferences in decision-making. Of course decision-making will embrace both the measurement and the valuation of risk changes and consequently if an individual refuses to accept that his assessment of the risk change is wrong then inevitably he will consider that it is not the measurement of risk that is being 'imposed' upon him but the valuation of the risk.

22

Whether we are right to assume as we have that individuals on the whole will be prepared in an area such as this to accept the state's (or its agents') judgments of estimation of risks as being in their own best interests—and therefore containable within the confines of consumer sovereignty—is extremely difficult to judge. If this judgment is wrong then our attempts to do so are but a false attempt to clothe our reasoning with an undeserved cloak of consumer sovereignty respectability. In this case we can simply accept Berlin's point and say that individuals are being 'coerced' for their own good which they are too blind to see and at the same time accept an element of paternalism.

But the issue need not remain wholly at an abstract level. If we look to the field of health care and the example of the doctor–patient relationship then is this not the supreme example of the state or its agent (in this case the doctor) 'imposing' knowledge on the individual? If my G.P. tells me that unless I have an operation there is a 50/50 chance that I will go blind, in deciding whether or not to have the operation I will almost certainly accept the G.P.'s judgment. Indeed although I may try to minimise the risk in my own mind I will be glad to be told on an 'expert' basis what the 'objective' level of risk is. Accepting this does not of course mean that if the doctor says I should have the operation that I ought yet again to accept the doctor's word. For we have now moved into the area of *valuation* of risk. For example it may be the case that there is (as assessed by the doctor again) a 1 in 1000 chance that I will die as a result of the operation. There therefore has to be a 'weighting' of a 50/50 chance of loss of sight against a 1 in 1000 chance of death. While the doctor may be in a position to tell me what the risks are he is in no position to tell me how I ought to weight risk of death against risk of blindness. If I am little concerned with losing my eyesight but have a great fear of death then I may well decide that I will not have the operation. What we have here therefore is the combination of a measurement of objective risk supplied by the state's representative and the consumer's sovereignty applying when the weights to be attached to different risks are being determined. This is the position which we would attempt to defend throughout this book. Thus while there may well be situations where it has to be accepted that we are dealing with cases of 'naked coercion' it does seem possible to defend the concept—in some cases at least—where consumers' sovereignty can embrace the idea of individuals allowing the state to make judgments on their behalf and doing so on the assumption that this is in their 'own best interests'.

2.5 CONCLUSION

In summary, this chapter has argued that the technique of cost-benefit analysis is a useful aid to decision-making in the public sector. Accepting this in those areas of policy concerned with life-saving and reductions in mortality means accepting that we need to establish values of life or of reductions in risk of death. By so doing decision-making in these areas will be made more rational and the return on investment in these areas increased. To state this is to state simply that the loss and anxiety associated with avoidable death in our society can be decreased in this way without any increase in the resources involved—and such is sufficient justification for wanting to determine the valuation of life or of reduction in risk of death.

The nature and philosophical basis of the appropriate social welfare function has been indicated and the principal elements of our liberal democratic traditions shown to be present in the form of social welfare functions proposed.

REFERENCES

1. Mishan, E. J., *Cost-Benefit Analysis*, George Allen and Unwin, London (1971)
2. Dasgupta, A. K., and Pearce, D. W., *Cost-Benefit Analysis: Theory and Practice*, Macmillan, London (1972)
3. Layard, R., *Cost Benefit Analysis: Selected Readings*, Penguin, Harmondsworth (1972)
4. Prest, A. R., and Turvey, R., Cost-benefit analysis: a survey, *Econ. J.*, 688, Dec. (1965)
5. Nash, C., Pearce, D., and Stanley, J., An evaluation of cost-benefit criteria, *Scot. J. Polit. Econ.*, **XXIII**, No. 2, June (1975)
6. Williams, A., The cost-benefit approach, *Br. Med. Bull.*, **30**, No. 3, 252 (1974)
7. Turvey, R., On the development of cost-benefit analysis. In *Cost Benefit Analysis*, Ed. M. G. Kendall, English Universities Press, London (1971)
8. Newton, T., *Cost Benefit Analysis in Administration*, Allen and Unwin, London, 230 (1972)
9. Weisbrod, B. A., *Economics of Public Health: Measuring the Economic Impact of Diseases*, Oxford University Press, London (1962)

10. Mill, J. S., *Essays on Ethics, Religion and Society, Works,* **X**, Toronto University Press, and Routledge and Kegan Paul, Toronto and London, 197–198 (1973)
11. Mill, J. S., *Utilitarianism, Liberty, Representative Government,* J. M. Dent & Sons, London, 132 (1972)
12. Berlin, I., Two concepts of liberty. In *Political Philosophy,* ed. A. Quinton, Oxford University Press, London, 141–152 (1967)

3

Life-saving Decision-making:
1 Road Safety

3.1 INTRODUCTION

3.1.1 *The Nature of Road Safety*

Some of the problems which exist in policy areas concerned with life saving are ones which are common to decision-making in the public sector generally. Others, however, are more specific. The types of problems which emerge and the nature of decision-making in life-saving activities are now discussed using the examples of road safety and health care, the former in this chapter and the latter in chapter 4.

The major component parts of road safety policy are as follows:

(1) Law and enforcement.
(2) Road construction, improvement and maintenance.
(3) Vehicle safety.
(4) Vehicle testing.
(5) Publicity, education and training.

The decision process in road safety is concerned to ensure the most effective deployment of resources to these different areas. Of course, resources are not necessarily wholly transferable from one area to the other (in the short run at least)—vehicle testers cannot become policemen overnight. None the less from the point of view of establishing some order of priority in terms of cost effectiveness initially at least they tend to be so considered.

Road safety is not an area of policy which can be considered in a compartment of its own. In so far as accidents do occur on the roads these can be viewed as part of the cost of travel. The gross benefits of transport are reduced to the extent that some disbenefits arise—accidents, noise, pollution, etc. As a society while we would accept that road accidents do represent a cost and that in some sense we would want to see this cost minimised, none the less we would not accept an objective of road safety policy as being to eliminate *all* accidents on the road. For example, one way that this could be achieved would be to ban all traffic from the roads. The cost of this would be such that there is little doubt that the overall welfare of society would be reduced—despite the current 7000 plus deaths annually on our roads.

This is not to say that the present level of deaths and injuries on our roads is in any sense optimal, although we are probably not so very far from an optimum position. For example, it is unlikely that the cost of reducing road accident deaths to 10 per cent of the current figure would be considered an improvement in total welfare by the majority of road users. To do so might require a road safety package which included such measures as compulsory wearing of car seat-belts; rigorously enforced speed limits of 30 m.p.h. everywhere; complete segregation of traffic from pedestrians; a statutorily binding obligation on parents not to allow children on the roads on their own, etc., etc. Similarly if road deaths rose to 50 000 per annum or even 20 000 per annum, there are grounds for believing that this would be considered an 'unacceptable' price for road transport and pressure would be applied to reduce the carnage on the roads.

3.1.2 *Decision-making in Road Safety*

Currently, it is extremely difficult to put any very precise figure on the resources devoted to road safety measures. The reasons for this are firstly that in such activities as road construction, road improvement and road maintenance benefits arise in various forms—accident savings, time and operating cost savings. For example estimating the proportion of the total cost of building a motorway which can be attributed to road safety is difficult if not impossible, except on a rather arbitrary basis. Secondly, in the case of vehicle safety, ideally what we want to measure is the difference in cost of a car with existing safety features as compared with a car which had no safety features. Even if we were in a position to estimate such a figure we would undoubtedly have problems with items like headlights which not only provide safety but other benefits in the form of allowing faster travel in the dark. Thirdly, in such cases as the training and testing of drivers we have no way of determining what proportion of the costs of these activities are attributable to the desire to be competent to drive as against the safety objective of being able to handle a vehicle in a reasonably safe manner. Thus there are major difficulties in determining just what the road safety budget comprises. Despite these difficulties and only by making some rather arbitrary assumptions it has been estimated that the resources devoted to road safety in the financial year 1970–71 were of the order of £400 million. While the accuracy of this estimate cannot be assessed it is sufficiently precise to indicate that the road safety 'industry' is quite sizeable.

Before being able to determine whether the road safety 'budget' is optimal in size we would need not only to be able to *value* the benefits of road safety policy—lives and injuries saved, damage to vehicles prevented, etc.—but also to be able to measure the effectiveness of current policy, in other words we would need to know the relevant existing production functions. In some areas of policy (for example vehicle-testing schemes) it is possible to obtain some indication of the cost of policies and their effect on accidents. But generally little information is available about the effectiveness of existing measures. Consequently on many existing problems we are in no position to even ask the question is it worth paying £y million to prevent x accidents, because while we may be able to get some reasonably accurate estimate of y, x is unknown. In such circumstances the question of valuing lives saved and other benefits does not arise. Unless we have some information about the effectiveness of a policy or measure then we cannot begin to apply cost-benefit analysis to decision-making in road safety.

Against this background and given the practical difficulties in trying to establish the effectiveness of measures introduced many years previously regarding past decisions we must let bygones be bygones. We can then proceed to ensure that *future* decisions are more scientifically based than their earlier counterparts. Even in looking for evidence that future measures have a known effectiveness we can run into difficulties. We may well find that before we can hope to forecast the future we need to be able to say something about the effectiveness of past measures. For example, a knowledge of the effectiveness of existing seat belts as worn by existing wearers is obviously important data in any decision process considering mechanical coercion or legal compulsion on belt-wearing. At the same time the situation is not static and we need to exercise care in using information based on current circumstances for forecasts of effectiveness in the future. In the case of seat belts one very important consideration is that of the nature of the two largely separate populations involved. Is it right to argue that current seat-belt wearers can be assumed to be a randomly selected group from those who will wear seat-belts under compulsion? This is unlikely. But can we argue that as regards the risk of being in an accident—obviously the most critical factor—the two populations can be considered identical. Whatever the answer the essential point here is that the evaluation process in road safety decision-making can only be effected on an explicit basis once a situation is reached in which the benefits of any policy option can be measured with some degree of accuracy (or ideally when we can say what the change is in the level of risk).

3.1.3 *Cost Effectiveness and Cost-benefit Analysis*

The use of cost-effectiveness techniques is now fairly widespread in road safety decision-making and it is becoming increasingly common to apply cost-benefit analysis using Dawson's[1,2] estimates for the valuation of the benefits (of which more in chapter 5, section 5.4.1). Aside from the question of the usefulness of these techniques as decision-making or aiding tools, one of the primary benefits of their use is in providing a useful framework for decision-making. Both techniques require an assembling of the relevant data in such a way that the cost of the measure can be set against the benefits in terms of accidents prevented, lives saved, injuries avoided, etc. Such a framework on its own is an important step forward.

Those cost-benefit analyses which are conducted on road safety policies do carry quite a considerable weight in the decision-making process. They can provide ammunition to back the administrators' views, but should these views and the ammunition prove to be on opposite sides it is quite possible that the cost-benefit conclusions will be overruled. Should the cost-benefit study be overwhelmingly for or against a particular policy on which the administrative decision-makers take an opposing view then of course the administrators will at the very least pause to consider the merits of the cost-benefit case. (After reflection they may still choose to reject the conclusions reached by C.B.A.) This may well be a very reasonable position to take in that both the economists and the administrators are aware that the existing method used for valuation of benefits of reduced injuries and deaths falls short of the ideal. Consequently the cost-benefit estimates in road safety are more tentative than they are in other fields.

One other aspect of these decision-making tools merits comment. Currently in estimating the benefits of any particular policy, these are measured in terms of numbers of fatal, serious and slight accidents or casualties. However, should we accept that the nature of the benefits to those principally concerned be in terms of reduced risk then we would need to convert the absolute numbers of savings in dead and injured to reductions in risk of death and in risk of injury. This is not just a matter of semantics. It raises fresh and interesting questions about valuation methodologies (as will be seen in chapters 8 and 9). At the same time it would mean that a broader data base would be required: no longer would it be sufficient to estimate savings in terms of 100 deaths and 800 injuries per annum; the population at risk would need to be known before the benefits could be converted to the form of reductions in risk of death and injury.

3.2 A CASE STUDY OF DECISION-MAKING: MOTORWAY BARRIERS

3.2.1 *The Background Study*

Rather than discuss the general problem of decision-making in road safety *in vacuo*—the pressure-group lobbying, the pressure of public opinion, the relationship of the economic decision process with the political etc. much useful understanding of the problem can be obtained from an account of the events and circumstances leading up to the decision to erect barriers on the central reserves of motorways to reduce 'cross-over' accidents. Following the decision reached and the policy laid down by the Ministry of Transport in 1967 (in other words, that it was the Ministry's intention to install crash barriers where traffic volumes were of the order of 40 000 vehicles a day or where particular road conditions made it desirable to do so) there was considerable political and public pressure applied to the Ministry to install crash barriers on all motorways. (The 40 000 figure was a 'best guess' at the time and had to be selected without the benefit of detailed investigation.)

As a result of this pressure a working party was set up to investigate the need for crash barriers on motorways. The working party was composed of engineers from the Ministry, members of the then Road Research Laboratory and economists. They found that the provision of safety fences in central reserves was widespread on the Continent and that the criteria for such provision were generally low or unrestrictive. In the United States application was dependent on traffic volumes but the criteria there lay between those on the Continent and those applying in this country. The working party was able to obtain an estimate of the effect of a central safety fence on accidents from a study of the accident record of two sections of a total length of 18 miles (28 km) on the M1 on which a safety fence had been erected in 1964. The accident record was compared with that of the remaining 38 miles (61 km) of the three-lane parts of the M1 for the two years 1962–63, when there was no central fence anywhere, and for the four years 1965–68 during which the fence was in use on the trial section. Accidents were classified in such a way that the effect of the presence of the barrier could be estimated. The accident experience on the trial section before the fence was installed and on the control section throughout the whole period were used to provide an estimate of the number, type and severity of the accidents which would have been expected on the section with the fences had they not been erected. The actual accident record was then compared with the expected record and the benefits determined using accident cost values calculated along the lines of Dawson[1,2] (see chapter 5, section 5.4.1). (It was estimated at that time that a fatal cross-over accident with collision cost £24 000, compared with £14 000 for an accident in which none of the vehicles crossed the reserve.) The estimated cost of each type of accident was applied to the difference between the observed and expected accidents of each type and the economic benefit of fencing thereby obtained. The total economic benefit over the four year period for the 18 mile stretch was estimated at £148 843, or £2067 per mile per year.

On the basis of the above evidence and calculations, the working party found that statistically there was a 70 per cent chance of the benefit lying between minus £2889 and plus £4219, the most likely estimate being plus £1864 per mile (or the £2067 figure above adjusted for a particular form of damage costs).

The working party—on the basis of some limited information —was able to establish estimates of the relative benefits of safety fences for differing volumes of traffic on dual two- and dual three-lane roads. Allowance was also made for estimating the growth of traffic

31

through time. On the basis of these calculations, the working party suggested the following criteria for minimum existing daily flows

Barriers to be provided at flow levels above:

	Average flow (vehicles per day)
Existing dual three-lane roads	25 000
Existing dual two-lane roads	17 500

The working party had reservations in accepting these criteria as the benefits were derived largely from the reduction of a small number of fatal accidents. Because of this and the fact that there was, on the basis of the evidence, a not insignificant chance that benefits might be negative, the working party concluded that barriers should only be introduced where the volume of traffic for dual three-lane roads was initially above 30 000 vehicles per day. Because of the reservations of the working party and the fact that their findings were open to some doubt, no immediate decision was made on their recommendations.

While the study was continuing and the recommendations being considered, several parliamentary questions were asked on the subject of barriers, mainly in terms of attempting to persuade the Government to construct more barriers. The pressure from press and public for an increased provision of barriers continued.

3.2.2 Reassessments

Between this time and a decision actually being taken in August 1970, in a review of accident cost valuation, the economists in the Ministry decide to revise their methodology (see Dawson[1,2]). The result of this revision was to increase markedly the cost of a fatal accident. In turn—since the benefit of barriers is activated largely through a reduction in fatal accidents with conceivably some offsetting increment in serious accidents—this meant that there was an increased return on the barriers as estimated by the working party (from a cost-benefit ratio of 3.3 to 4.2 and from a first-year rate of return of 17.6 per cent to 23.4 per cent for a dual three-lane road with 30 000 vehicles per day).

The reassessment of the benefits on these lines was made in July 1970. Early in August a resubmission on barriers was sent to Ministers. In the meantime largely as a result of several particularly serious accidents resulting in multiple deaths and which involved vehicles crossing the central reserve of a motorway, there was increased pressure from various organisations and particularly from the press for the government to take action to erect barriers on all motorways.

Late in August the Minister issued the following statement

'Following a thorough review by my Department of the need for crash barriers on the central reserves of motorways, I have decided that such barriers are to be installed. This will be a big task but the aim would be to install barriers on the busiest motorways, including the M1 to Birmingham, by the end of 1971, and complete the installation on about 1000 miles by 1975.'

3.2.3 *Discussion*

This particular example is noteworthy for several reasons. The type of situation which arose with barriers is not an uncommon one in road safety. A particular type of accident could be easily identified both by its nature and its location and an (apparent) solution was readily at hand. The pressure for action, although undoubtedly well-intentioned, was not based solely on reason nor on the full facts. There were many possible solutions (at least partial) to the problem with which barriers were designed to cope (for example, increasing width of central reserve). In turn there were several types of barrier—all with different effects and different costs.

A further complication—and one of some considerable concern at the time—was that benefits from the installation of barriers were of a somewhat peculiar nature. Firstly, in some circumstances, barriers can increase the level of risk if a vehicle enters the central reserve. This is particularly true at low traffic volumes, when the probability that a vehicle will enter the reserve, cross it and hit another vehicle is small. The risk of serious accidents occurring may well be increased if barriers are erected. The vehicle will then enter the reserve and do one of three things: (a) strike the barrier and stay on the reserve; (b) strike the barrier and come back on to the same carriageway again without striking another vehicle; and (c) strike the barrier, come back and strike another vehicle. (In very few cases the vehicle will actually go through the barrier.) Where traffic volumes are low the risk of a serious accident may well be higher than if the vehicle had not been

33

'protected' by a barrier. Secondly there is the possibility that drivers suffer from 'barrier shyness' which may or may not be a desirable thing from a safety standpoint but is certainly not desirable from a traffic flow or capacity point of view. Thirdly, while barriers do tend to reduce the number of fatal accidents (and certainly the number of fatalities per fatal accident) they can increase the number of serious non-fatal accidents. There is thus a trade-off between a few deaths prevented and a more substantial increase in serious injuries.

Now the basis of most of the pressure for the installation of barriers was simply (a) that these accidents of considerable severity appeared to be occurring with alarming frequency; and (b) that a readily available solution could be implemented, namely install barriers. What in actual fact was a very complex issue could be presented in straightforward black-and-white terms: the government was dragging its feet.

This example serves to indicate the combination of factors affecting decision-making in road safety. Since the example raises a number of points which are relevant to the description of the social welfare function and the decision rules to be applied to public sector project appraisal we will return to it in chapter 9.

3.3 CONCLUSION

Cost-benefit analysis is already an important tool in road safety decision-making. However, before its full potential can be realised it would be necessary for firstly the economist practitioners and secondly the administrative and political decision-makers to be convinced, not only of the merit and the validity of the techniques involved as they currently are, but also of the valuation procedures employed. Both these groups appreciate the limitations of the valuation methods used at present; and as a result cost benefit has had a more tentative impact in road safety decision-making than, for example, it has had in decision-making in road-building and improvement. There the acceptability of using values of time has been more firmly established and this largely because of the much sounder base on which these time-values are based. What is clear from this is that it is not enough to improve the methodology of valuation of life and limb to the satisfaction of academic economists—although this is of obvious importance—what is also essential is to convince the administrative and political decision-makers that the improved methodology is valid and consequently it is also essential to be able to explain the basis of the methodology in terms which the non-economist can understand.

REFERENCES

1. Dawson, R. F. F., *Cost of Road Accidents in Great Britain*, Road Research Laboratory (1967)
2. Dawson, R. F. F., *Current Costs of Road Accidents in Great Britain*, Road Research Laboratory (1971)

4

Life-saving Decision-making:
2 Health Care

4.1 SOME PROBLEMS IN APPLYING C.B.A. TO HEALTH CARE

As was remarked above one of the principal reasons for the lack of impact of C.B.A. in health care is that decision-makers in health have tended, with some considerable justification, to scorn the 'man as a machine' type of valuation. This, possibly more than any other reason, has resulted in a disillusionment with C.B.A. as applied to the allocation of resources within the health sector. Economists operating in that sector—and they remain a small and relatively ineffectual band (at least at the level of their impact on decision-making)—have significantly failed as yet to improve upon the 'human capital' valuation approach. What does seem central to the issue of cost benefit analysis having any real impact in the health sector is that, as in all areas of life saving, until economists can improve upon the methodology of valuation it is unlikely that health decision-makers will look to economists for help and guidance in resource allocation questions, except of course where essentially operations research techniques or cost-effectiveness studies can be of some help.

A second feature which prevents a more rational look at resource allocation in this field is that the growth of the National Health Service (N.H.S.) has seen little if any diminution in the power of the medical profession and only very little awareness of the possible need to restrict their power. It is perhaps as well to state immediately that the decision-making with which we are here concerned is in terms of relatively broad questions of resource allocation and certainly not with any direct interference with medical judgment. What has to be said however is that there is no reason to believe (and considerable reason

36

to doubt) that medical personnel are in the best position to determine how resources should be distributed. This requires a much broader view than can be achieved by medical specialists trying to outshout each other in an attempt to win as great a share of the cake as *they* believe their particular specialty requires. Inevitably any change in the deployment of resources will affect the framework within which the professionals must operate and make decisions. Questions of priorities based on economic principles will almost always be concerned with establishing the right framework and not with interfering with clinical freedom within that framework.

Thirdly, decision-making in health care is very diffuse. Not only is some power devolved from the Department of Health and Social Security to the Regions, thence to the Areas, thence to the Districts but within a district or even a hospital the number of individuals who are involved in resource allocation questions in different ways is very great. This can create problems for the analyst in knowing who it is who requires advice and how it is that final decisions on resource allocation emerge. Add to this the fact that some of those working 'on the shop floor'—the medical personnel—are the most highly paid, and we can see that we do not have a normal pyramid of a decision-making system in the health service.

Fourthly, the nature of the output of the health services is also particularly diffuse. While there does not appear to be any study which has attempted to reveal it (and it is perhaps impossible to arrive at a quantitative answer anyway) it is likely that the proportion of total N.H.S. resources which is directed towards the saving of life is quite small. Even where outputs can be identified in terms of lives saved (in screening for breast cancer, for example) a considerable amount of output will take the form of reduced morbidity, less pain, improved care and comfort, etc. Measurement of these outputs is likely to prove very tricky and evaluation more difficult even than that of lives saved.

Fifthly, even if we could achieve some conceptual framework in which to measure and evaluate health outputs, in considering particular diseases and different forms of treatment it is frequently difficult if not impossible to determine how effective treatment is. Much of what passes for medical practice today has never been subject to any form of genuine appraisal but has become established with the passage of time. While most of these practices probably do result in some improvement or easing of the patient's condition, it is

37

relatively common to find doctors who have little faith in the effectiveness of at least some forms of treatment. Where the real problem lies is that frequently once it is established that a particular service or form of treatment yields some level of positive benefit (no matter how small) it then becomes 'unethical' to mount randomised trials to determine the extent of the effectiveness because this would involve deliberately *not* giving some patients the better form of treatment.

Sixthly, there has, until recent times, been little call for this type of analysis in the health care sector. This would seem to have its roots in the thinking which surrounded the setting up of the N.H.S. where it was thought that with the passage of time there would be a withering away of the state of ill-health with a concurrent reduction in the need to be concerned with resource allocation problems since these would be made in a climate of much-reduced demand. Today, given the increased expectations of good health as well as such factors as the growth of new diseases, this is obviously a pipe dream but one which has been relatively slow to be recognised as such. As a result we are now faced with a juggernaut of an N.H.S. for which the examination of its direction of travel and the contents of its load are long overdue.

Thus other than the issue of the methodological problems there are good reasons why health care has been largely neglected by economists. But is there anything that can be done about it from a methodological standpoint? Can concepts and approaches which are appropriate to road safety and valuation of life there have any real bearing in the health sector? Are there differences in approach required for each sector considered or can the methodologies of valuation of life generally be transferred more or less as they stand to the health field or any other policy area involving life saving?

4.2 A CASE STUDY IN DECISION-MAKING: SCREENING FOR CERVICAL CANCER

4.2.1 *The Nature of the Problem*

An example of the type of decision in health care which embodies some of the problems raised above is that of the screening programme for cervical cytology. Considerable publicity has been given to the view that cervical cancer can be detected at the *in situ* stage. It is also claimed that *in situ* cancer in at least some instances progresses to invasive cancer and thence to death. By treating the cancer at the *in situ* stage it may be possible to prevent the invasive cancer and thereby avoid some premature deaths.

Now in such circumstances as these the questions faced by Department of Health and Social Security (D.H.S.S.) officials and the medical profession are: ought we to have a mass-screening programme for cervical cancer? If so, which women should be screened? And again how frequently should screening take place? There are considerable gaps in the medical knowledge of the disease but there are three pointers which can be used to identify the groups of women most at risk

(a) Age—the prevalence increases with age.
(b) Social class—there is a positive correlation with social class (that is, social class IV and V are most at risk).
(c) Number of children borne—multiparous women are more susceptible.

Assuming that sufficient knowledge existed as to the natural history of the disease and the efficiency of screening in detecting true positives and true negatives and that effective treatment was available, then given knowledge of the three factors (a), (b) and (c) above estimates could then be made of the 'yield' of screening different groups of women at different frequencies. Assuming that the 'yield' was measured in terms of 'lives saved', and that the cost per woman screened is constant and known, then we can envisage a 'supply curve' of lives which is subject to diminishing returns. For example, assuming a constant response rate in all groups we might find that (if all groups were equal in numbers) the order of priority for screening would be

(i) Women over 35, in social class IV and V with three or more children.
(ii) Women over 35, in social class IV and V with less than three children.
(iii) Women over 35 in social class I, II and III with three or more children.
(iv) Women age 25–35 in social class IV and V with three or more children.
(v) Women over 35 in social class IV and V with three or more children and screened five years previously.

39

4.2.2 *Measuring Costs and Benefits*

While the ordering of the above is arbitrary it may not be too far removed from the true situation had we all the medical facts required. If we assume for simplicity that the cost of treatment following screening is equal to the cost of treatment which would have been incurred later had the women in the absence of screening, presented symptomatically, then the cost per life saved is in inverse proportion to the number of positive cases found per 1000 women screened. (This only holds if the cost per woman screened is constant and the effectiveness of treatment is constant across all groups of women.) For example let us assume (a) that treatment is 100 per cent effective (women treated following a positive finding never die of cervical cancer but otherwise would); (b) the cost per women screened is £1; and (c) the positive rate per million women screened in groups (i) to (v) above is 100, 70, 50, 35 and 24. Then the 'cost per life saved' in each of these five groups of 1 million women is £10 000 (that is, £1 × 1 million ÷ 100), £14 300, £20 000, £28 600 and £41 700 respectively.

This example is much simplified. (It also supposes that the medical data are available to allow such calculations to be made; currently they are not.) But it brings out the essential problem of decision-making in this and similar areas. The two-part question which has to be answered is: which women, if any, should be screened and how often? As we extend the programme to lower-risk women so the cost per life saved increases. Indeed we could redefine the problem in such

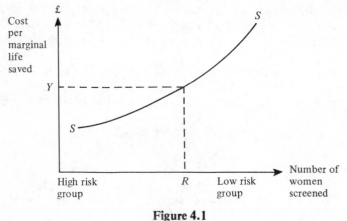

Figure 4.1

a way as to obtain a more or less continuous 'supply curve' as shown in figure 4.1.

Now once it has been decided to set in motion a programme which involves the screening of some women, from a purely medical position there is no obvious place to stop along this continuous curve. The only medically 'best' solution is to screen all women at possibly six-monthly (or even three-monthly) intervals. Obviously this solution is a non-starter because of the cost involved. Yet a decision has to be made—because resources are scarce—which will mean that some women at risk are not screened and therefore (in terms of our assumptions above) some deaths from cervical cancer will still occur which might be avoided through screening.

4.2.3 Discussion

This issue can be resolved in a rational sense in one of only two ways. Either a decision has to be made *ex cathedra* that the total resources to be devoted to the screening programme be £x million per annum. Where x is given then we bring cost-effectiveness techniques to bear on the problem by attempting to maximise the number of lives saved from this budget. Alternatively a decision has to be taken that no more than £y should be spent on saving a life in which case given the curve in figure 4.1 the screening programme should cater for all groups to the left of point R but not those to the right.

What this example signifies is that while decisions are made with regard to the size and scope of such a screening programme they tend to be taken as isolated decisions and little if any attempt is made to estimate the 'opportunity cost' (or benefit foregone) from devoting scarce resources to this particular project at the expense of losing the benefits which the same resources might have yielded elsewhere. While the medical profession may attempt to maximise the return on investment *within* the area of cervical cancer screening (although some doubts must exist as to whether this occurs, despite its narrow context) what can be said with little fear of contradiction is that decisions on such issues as these are not even conceived within the type of framework which would allow truly rational decisions to be made.

41

4.3 WHOSE VALUES IN HEALTH CARE?

4.3.1 *The Nature of Health Care Demand*

In the case of health care by and large the only real choices open to the individual are whether or not to make initial demands on the health service by presenting himself at the G.P.'s surgery and whether he drops out at any stage of treatment or goes through with it. Generally the nature of the health care supplied is not something which the individual consumer is in a position to influence or possibly feel that he is in a position to judge. This provides us with an insight into what it is we might consider as the 'good' in the case of health. The consumer is not-concerned with whether his G.P. gives him a pat on the back, a bottle of pills or a week in bed for an operation. What he is concerned with is (a) that when he is in a state of ill-health he is returned to as good a state of health as possible as quickly as possible; (b) that when he is in a state of good health the risk of moving to a state of ill-health at any time is minimised; and (c) that he is reassured that should his state of health (or ill-health) become such that he requires treatment then the necessary treatment will be available.

The demand for health can be seen as a 'derived' demand. There seems little value in health *per se*; the value lies in the things that can be done because we are in good health. Put differently, the disutility of ill-health arises from being constrained from leading a full life because of pain or handicap or some other disability. The demand for health care can be considered as 'derived' in a further sense. This arises because individuals are normally concerned with a return to health and are content to (or have to?) leave it to others—the medical profession—to determine what health care services they require. (See Grossman[1] for a fuller discussion of the nature of health care demand.)

We might therefore contend that had we a measure of the value to individuals of being able to participate in life to the full—subject to all constraints other than ill-health—then the extent to which ill-health interfered with this could provide a measure of the disutility of ill-health. In the case of death of course the ill-health constraint is absolute and there will be various gradations in this constraint between death and perfect health (however defined). However no measure of this 'value of living'—for that is what it is—exists and, it can be argued, nor is it likely to. Individuals would almost certainly

42

have difficulties in attempting to comprehend and thereafter form judgments as to the value of living or the value of not being restricted in their activities. The choices involved are basically too awesome. More important however they are not the choices faced by the majority of individuals. Those of us who are in reasonably good health do not face a probability of one of death or incapacity—except of course in the long run. What we are more likely to be concerned with is a probability of very much less than one—some small *risk* of death or incapacity. We do not actually hear the bell tolling for us, but we are aware that there is some probability that it will.

With regard to these probabilities what stance ought we to take on the question of perception? Normally the individual himself is not in a position to judge the size of the risk he faces and almost certainly never in a position to gauge the reduction in risk through treatment. At present most of the areas of health decision-making are 'handed over' to the state and the medical profession. This means in effect that not only are the questions of risk levels settled by others but the *valuation* of health benefits is likewise determined. As previously argued while the state and the medical profession are without doubt better placed to determine what the relevant risk levels are and the effectiveness of different treatments in reducing these risk levels, it is difficult to see how one could argue that they are better placed than the individual to determine the value of benefits.

4.3.2 Two Other Types of Demand

There is however a different type of demand other than a probabilistic one for health care, and that is for the present sick who currently require health care. Since the purpose of estimating values and the demand for health is eventually to provide guide-lines for the allocation of resources within (and possibly also to) the health field, we probably need not concern ourselves overmuch with the estimation of demand of the present short-term sick, since the lag in adjustment on the supply side will be greater than the time-period in which this group are ill. (The definition of short term here can be determined if we can establish what the relevant lags are on the supply side.) This does not, however, solve the problem of the long-term sick, such as the handicapped (both physical and mental). While there seems no obvious way of fitting these groups into the probabilistic approach suggested above for the current well it is possible that what might

43

emerge from any estimation of demand by the well would provide guide-lines for the treatment of demand by the current long-term sick.

Despite what has been said about the demand for health care *vis-à-vis* the demand for health, there may be in fact an element of more direct demand for health care provision. This is based on the concept of 'option demand' which is discussed in detail in chapter 8. There it is argued that in the case of a privately owned hospital, while the revenue obtained through the treatment of patients might not be sufficient to keep the hospital open, the well in the area of the hospital might be prepared to pay towards the financing of the hospital simply because they want the hospital to be there in the event that they require its services. Such an argument suggests that these two components—value in use and value in anticipation—are both relevant to the decision on whether to keep the hospital open or not.

4.3.3 *The Relevance of the Consumer's Views*

Turning now to the valuation methodology *per se*, we have stated previously that we are interested in individuals' evaluations of the effects of health care accruing to them. There are two points here: firstly that the individual is capable of making the necessary judgments involved; and secondly that the individual is the appropriate judge of the weight or importance to be attached to particular factors. Both points have tended to be ignored to date in valuation issues because the question of consumer preferences has not arisen. The valuation system used has been by and large an 'imposed' system, largely based on 'health as an investment' along the lines of the method which is outlined in chapter 5. (The case studies there of Klarman[2], Weisbrod[3], and Rice and Cooper[4] are all concerned with the health output evaluation problem.) At the moment it seems unlikely that a situation will be reached where individuals will be able to determine the extent and nature of provision of health care in the same way and to the same extent that they do in the case of striped toothpaste. What can be argued is that decision-makers in health care ought to be concerned with what individuals' demand for health is, and going further ought to base their decisions at least in part on a reflection of individuals' demand. To argue that the individual is incapable of making the appropriate judgments would of course immediately kill the concept of introducing any element of consumers' sovereignty. There may well be areas where this is true

44

and we need to define very closely which judgments we are concerned with here. This is closely linked to the question of whether the individual is the appropriate judge of the weight or importance attached to particular factors. It is not suggested that the individual—apart from the concept of option demand—will be in a position to make judgments as to the provision of different types of health care. What is suggested is that the individual is capable of making decisions and is the relevant decision-maker regarding the question of how much health (as opposed to health services) ought to be provided and at what 'price'. Viewed in these terms there is no suggestion that individuals would be left to decide what form of treatment they should receive. Decisions regarding the type of treatment can be left to the medical profession as at present.

What the above has served to indicate is that although there are various different problems in the application of our methodology to the field of health output evaluation nonetheless there appears to be no reason why it could not be applied to this field as well. If the good 'health' is defined in a certain way then it ought to be possible to bring the techniques of cost-benefit analysis to bear on decision-making in this area. If, however, we continue to accept that the whole (or virtually the whole) of health service decision-making should be left to the 'experts' then of course there is no need to concern ourselves with individuals' preferences. But is the supply of health services not too important a matter to be left to the suppliers? *Quis custodiet ipsos custodies?*

4.4 CONCLUSION

We have emphasised the philosophy of consulting the potential sufferers when determining the values to be placed on such matters as lives saved, injury avoided and morbidity reduced. As a result we can confidently argue that the cost-benefit framework suggested for obtaining values—as depicted in chapter 2—can be applied to the field of health benefits.

However, there are problems in applying the methodology to health care partly because of the nature of the good 'health' and partly because of the way in which it is supplied.

While it might be of interest to look at other fields in which life savings form part of the output and determine yet again whether the approach applies to these, it is most likely that it will. Undoubtedly the type of problems of application which we have discussed in the health sector may well apply in other areas—and other new application problems may arise. Nonetheless the methodology is likely to have common usage in all sectors where the problem of life valuation arises—fire prevention, air–sea rescue services, mountain rescue teams, building structures regulations, etc. In many of these areas the problems associated with quantifying the effectiveness of ameliorative measures are as difficult if not more so than in the examples of road safety and health care. But this does not undermine the usefulness of having explicit values of life to measure the worth of some investment in these areas. At the present time there is little incentive to attempt to quantify benefits and costs in these areas. If a situation should develop such that it were possible to calculate the benefit of saving a life this would create considerable pressure to quantify the impact of the different policies available and assist in determining the priority to be given to any particular project.

APPENDIX TO CHAPTER 4—HEALTH INDICATORS

While discussing the problems of decision-making in the health sector it is worth looking briefly at the relationship between what has been said above and 'health indicators'. In this instance the example of Culyer, Lavers and Williams[5] is used. Of particular interest in their study is the question of *whose* values are used in determining the various measures required in health indicators.

Firstly with regard to 'state-of-health' indicators, Culyer *et al.* argue that we need to try to see 'if there is any consensus among medical personnel as to how painful and how restricting particular conditions are'. Thereafter they suggest that the relative weights to be attached to pain and restriction should be 'essentially a social judgment and should be recognised as such'; they add however that such judgments 'may have to be made in practice by medical people'. They continue that as regards 'society's judgments concerning the relative importance of avoiding one state rather than another' (that is, statements regarding health policy) these should be made 'by whoever is entrusted with that responsibility—for example "The Minister"'. On duration of illness, they argue that this is a straightforward problem which can be 'cast in statistical terms'—which means in their interpretation that ten people suffering from condition A for one week is equivalent to one person suffering from condition A for ten weeks.

They add, however, that 'the satisfaction felt by patients themselves (or their friends and relatives) is not regarded as an independent consideration in this formulation' and further that 'to do so would raise such enormous difficulties for any health indicator that the matter is mentioned here only so that it is not lost sight of'.

On the meaning of need, Culyer *et al.* argue that 'the agent responsible for the decision ('the Minister') should attach explicit *valuations* to a variety of levels of the state indicator'. Finally the authors confess that 'the difficulty with the cost-benefit notion of need is that it requires that the properties of the social welfare function be identified in the relevant range'. On the measurement of need indicators, they point to the use by the Department of the Environment of explicit values of human lives and suggest that progress is being made towards the solution of the difficulties involved in this area.

Taken together, Culyer *et al.* appear to argue that the social welfare function is by and large an imposed one—albeit imposed by the Minister—although it is possible to see within their formulation the signs of a more truly consumer preference-based social welfare function. The formulation proposed in chapters 2 and 4 would differ from the Culyer *et al.* line to the extent that

(1) The trade-off between pain and restriction ought to be based on social, that is, individual consumers', preferences. (They may be right that in practice this trade-off has to be made by medical people but this would only be acceptable if it transpired that consumers were incapable of making the trade-offs.)

(2) Judgments concerning the relative importance of avoiding one state as against another ought to be based on consumers' preferences. (Certainly there will almost always be an element of political decision-making but the value judgment can be made that the Minister's decision ought to reflect consumers' preferences as far as possible regarding the weights attached to avoiding one state rather than another. *How* the states are avoided is a matter for medical and political judgment.)

(3) The duration question ought again to be based on consumers' preferences. While the strictly linear approach suggested by Culyer *et al. may* turn out to be the right one, if consumers' preferences reveal some different relationships then this ought to be used.

(4) The satisfaction felt by patients themselves (or their relatives

and friends) ought to be the basis for determining the weights to be attached to different outcomes—in terms of *final* outcomes. Such satisfactions are not relevant to the determination of the required inputs to achieve these final outcomes.

(5) Ideally the consumers ought to be the valuers in determining the explicit valuations to be placed on a variety of levels of the 'state-of-health' indicator—again defined in terms of *final* output.

(6) The definition of the properties of the social welfare function in the relevant range is difficult as Culyer *et al.* suggest but unless we are content to continue with an imposed social welfare function then attempts must be made to bring consumers' preferences to bear on that social welfare function. This is central to all that has been said in chapter 4.

It may well be that Culyer *et al.* are being realistic in their assessment of who the relevant decision-makers should be regarding different areas of decision. It is also true that their approach if successful leads to a more rational allocation of resources than is the case at present. It is unlikely however to proceed very far (as it stands) in introducing a more consumer-oriented preference system into the implicit (or explicit) health social welfare function. Under their approach it would remain—as now—largely imposed (albeit by benevolent political and administrative decision-makers). We are very much on virgin territory in making any attack on this area of introducing the concepts of consumer demand, consumers' surplus and cost-benefit analysis into the decision process in health care. Such attacks may well result in some painful processes, not only in terms of the problems of making advances on the methodological front but also, if advances are to be made, in persuading those concerned that it is right and proper that the recipients of the services should have some say in determining the weights and values to be placed on the final outcomes.

REFERENCES

1. Grossman, M., On the concept of health capital and the demand for health, *J. Polit. Econ.*, **80**, No. 2, 223 (1972)
2. Klarman, H. E., Syphilis control programs. In *Measuring Benefits of Government Investments*, ed. R. Dorfman, Brookings Institute, Washington (1965)

3. Weisbrod, B. A., *Economics of Public Health*, University of Pennsylvania Press, Philadelphia (1961)
4. Rice, D. P., and Cooper, B. S., The economic value of human life, *Amer. J. Public Health*, **57**, No. 11, 1954 (1967)
5. Culyer, A. J., Lavers, R., and Williams, A., *Social indicators—health*. In *Social Trends*, HMSO, London (1971)

5

The Accounting or Human Capital Approach to Life Valuation

5.1 INTRODUCTION

In this chapter and chapter 6 various methods for valuing life are considered. These tend to be methods which have been used, are being used or have been proposed at different times, with at least some realisation that they fall short of the ideal. In considering these methods from a conceptual and theoretical standpoint it is important not to lose sight of the need to obtain actual values, that is, put the methods into practice. Consequently we need to be wary of dismissing methods too readily which, although perhaps not ideal in theory, may at least be capable of improving upon the allocation of resources in life-saving activities and at the same time capable of yielding actual values. In this and the next chapter various studies are quoted to indicate how the approaches have been or could be applied. These are not intended to be comprehensive but are used merely as examples.

5.2 THE CONCEPT OF HUMAN CAPITAL

5.2.1 *Definition of Human Capital*

There is now a wealth of literature available on what is termed in economic theory 'investment in man', 'human capital' or 'human wealth'. This section will not provide a full account of all the theory and its ramifications, but will give sufficient background to allow the reader to consider the applicability of the theory to the valuation of human life in the next section. (For those interested in obtaining a deeper knowledge of the theory of human capital see for example Schultz[1] and Becker[2].)

Economists have long been aware that man ought not to be considered in the economic system purely in terms of his being one unit in a homogeneous labour force. Indeed in the writings of Adam Smith[3] in the eighteenth century this awareness was already apparent. In much of the intervening two centuries however economists have frequently chosen to avoid the 'complications' which acceptance of this concept might mean. Largely as a result of this, the concept of human capital has been slow to develop and the necessary theoretical, analytical and applied work required for the concept to gain acceptance even slower.

Schultz[1], probably the leading exponent of the concept, provides the basic simple proposition on which the whole edifice of human capital theory rests, namely 'that people enhance their capabilities as producers and as consumers by investing in themselves'. Becker[2] suggests that 'activities that influence future monetary and psychic income by increasing the resources in people ... are called investments in human capital'. The areas in which we find this concept being applied most frequently are in education, health and training. When the state or an individual (or any economic agency for that matter) decides to invest, the decision to be made entails a choice between present and future consumption. All other things being equal, given the choice between having something sooner rather than later, most of us would choose to have it sooner. There is an opportunity cost of waiting. Consequently before being induced to wait, most of us would look for some compensation either in terms of a positive inducement now or in terms of a higher benefit in the future. This principle which is central to the economic theory of investment is also applicable to investment in human capital. For example, undergraduates forego present earnings while at university in the expectation of obtaining higher earnings in the future through their investment in education.

5.2.2 *Some Problems of Comprehensiveness*

But the concept of human capital is not without its opponents. Schultz accepts that opposition is common. He suggests that most of it stems from a feeling that there is something morally and/or ethically wrong in treating man as some sort of capital—a concept previously ascribed only to machines, buildings, and other 'things'. Without going too deeply into the argument at this stage it is sufficient to state that the concept *can* be divorced from moral and ethical considerations.

Human capital theory is principally concerned, not with anything as abstract as the quality of life or the value of life, but with the value of changes in the quantity and quality of labour. It embodies in essence an acceptance—indeed rationalisation—of the heterogeneous nature of labour. It further accepts that investments in education, health etc., can and do have an effect on the quality of labour (and also the quantity in certain instances). It argues that these effects can be distinguished from inherent or 'natural' ability or capacity and therefore that measurements can be made of the effects of the different inputs into human capital. Although in the face of some criticism attempts have been made to widen the base of human capital theory, such attempts have tended to result in more befogging of the issue of what human capital is all about. Let us content ourselves with Schultz's[1] approach: 'My treatment of education will in no way detract from, or disparage, the cultural contributions of education. It takes these contributions for granted and proceeds to the task of determining whether there are also some economic benefits from education that may be treated as capital that can be identified and estimated'.

But the argument is further complicated by the possible existence of consumption benefits arising at the time of and in the very act of investing. For example, is it not the case that most undergraduates obtain some benefit during the period when society—and themselves—are investing in their further education? These complications mean that any study of human capital is bound to be bedevilled by problems of measurement. What are justifiably considered to be the investment costs? To what extent are such decisions human-capital motivated (as opposed to present-consumption motivated)? Have all the benefits from the investment been included—and at the right point in time? Are all the monetary benefits (and costs) included—and how are these to be valued? All these are very real problems which although not fundamental to the concept of human capital, none the less create sufficiently sizeable difficulties to raise a few questionmarks over the concept—at least at the level of its being a useful tool in applied economics.

More fundamentally the problem of investment in human capital requires *a priori* a treatment which in its own terms of reference the approach used at present cannot adequately provide. To quote

Becker[4] in one study on education: 'A treatment of the full, as opposed to the economic, social rate of return on college education would involve a consideration of cultural advance, democratic government, etc. and is clearly far beyond the scope of this study'. And again from the same source[4]: 'Quantitative estimates of psychic gains are never directly available and are usually computed residually as the difference between independent estimates of monetary and real gains'. From the point of view of any policy implications of their studies the proponents of human capital theory would argue that the inclusion of cultural factors in, for example, a study of education would have the effect of raising the rate of return. Thus if the calculations of human capitalists yield positive returns the result can normally be taken as a lower limit estimation. Where greater problems arise, of course, is when—as is more frequently the case—the choice is not simply that of deciding 'yes' or 'no' for a particular project but making a choice between several competing projects. If it were the case that the relationship between the quantified economic benefits and the unquantified other benefits were constant, then this would be a comparatively minor problem. In some cases it has been argued (see for example Weisbrod's[5] treatment of valuation of life from a human capital standpoint) that such a relationship is sufficiently constant (or in Weisbrod's case the profile by age for the two types of benefit is sufficiently similar) for the assumption to hold good. In many instances this assumption is likely to prove difficult to support.

To point to this problem is, of course, only to raise a difficulty familiar to all those who at any time have been concerned with the use of cost-benefit analysis in decision-making. Frequently it is not possible to place a monetary value on all the benefits likely to flow from a particular decision or for that matter, on all the costs. As a result of this, cost-benefit analysis has been criticised as being guilty of over-emphasising the quantifiable at the expense of the 'intangible'. In the same way that cost-benefit analysts would argue in defence that their brief is to reduce the area of uncertainty, and where necessary leave the political processes to value the intangibles, so the human capital theorist would argue that he is quantifying some of the benefits and that the remainder, of which he is fully aware, must be valued by others. The essential point in this is that the boundaries of the expertise of the human capital analysts are, or ought to be, fairly narrowly defined.

53

5.2.3 *A Conceptual Difficulty*

One other aspect of human capital theory is worth mentioning. This is that frequently inputs to human capital are financed by the state, the National Health Service, the compulsory and largely state-financed educational system, etc. and there are a number of reasons for this. However what is of most immediate relevance is the suggestion that left to themselves individuals are much less likely than is society to invest optimally in human capital, and further that this 'non-optimality' will be on the side of the too-little rather than the too-much. This raises extremely interesting questions about how one sets about valuation, attempting to use a consumer sovereignty base, when a part at least of the rationality of the provision of the good in question is that individual judgment is poor to the extent that this poverty of judgment is frequently considered sufficient justification for taking the judgment out of the individual's hands and placing it in the hands of society or its agents. How can we attempt seriously to apply the consumer sovereignty principle to *compulsory* education? How do we measure the relative benefits of regular haemodialysis as against kidney transplant when only the medical profession and the unfortunate (or fortunate?) few who have experienced these treatments are truly in a position to say what the effects are? These are difficulties which we will consider in more detail at a later point.

5.3 THE APPLICATION OF HUMAN CAPITAL THEORY TO VALUATION OF LIFE

5.3.1 *The Determination of Human Capital Life Values*

Turning more directly now to the application of the human capital school of thought to the valuation of life, we find that this type of methodology is the one that has dominated valuation of life as far back at least as Sir William Petty[6] in the seventeenth century and which today is more familiar in the writings of Weisbrod[5,7], Klarman[8], Dublin and Lotka[9], Dawson[10,11], etc. The principle involved, as we might expect from the above account of the nature of the human capital theory, is simply that of valuing life in terms of the value of labour. Given adequate data regarding lifetime earnings, participation rates in the labour force, mortality rates, etc., it is possible to estimate the value of the expected future earnings of individuals in any age-group. On the somewhat heroic assumption that wage rates are a precise indicator of productivity then the same measure—with perhaps some adjustment to allow for social preferences being different from private preferences—can be used às a measure of the value of the future output of the individual to society, in other words the 'social value'. The values emerging are usually referred to as the 'economic values of life' and mention is normally made of the fact that this of course only reflects that part of the valuation of life which is capable of quantification, there being other 'non-economic' or 'intangible' aspects which are additional to that part of life which the method has been able to measure. This type of valuation system is the one most commonly found in practice.

The standard format for the approach can be built up as follows. If an individual is saved from death at a particular moment in time, then thereafter he will continue to be a producer. What he produces is of value to the community and consequently we can equate his value with the value of his output. Earnings are normally assumed to be a fairly accurate estimate of the value of this output.

Consequently the individual's stream of future earnings represents his 'human capital' value. The earnings figures used can be national average earnings as a first approximation or allowance can be made for age profiles of earnings. Again if it were thought justified to differentiate between high and low wage earners (for example, if we were concerned with car safety, car drivers' earnings are higher than the national average) then the appropriate earnings figures could be used.

In estimating earnings levels in the future an allowance is normally made for the expected growth in real earnings through time and this is built into the calculation of the future earnings stream. The fact that individuals may be unemployed at various periods in their working life can be accounted for by applying to the earnings stream the appropriate age-adjusted labour force participation rates. A further adjustment is made for mortality rates since we cannot assume that the individual will necessarily live until his normal retirement date.

Finally the adjusted stream of life-time earnings has to be 'discounted' to convert it to 'present value' terms. This simply means that the value at the present time of earnings in the future is less than similar earnings now. (This is not a question of inflation. It arises because of uncertainty about individuals' survival, positive economic growth rates, and a pure time preference concept—we prefer things now rather than later. The concept of discounting is discussed in detail in appendix B). This present value stream of future earnings, with these various adjustments made, then represents the 'human capital' value of life.

To allow for the valuation of housewives' lives, an imputed wage can be assessed for housewives and the procedure as outlined above then applied. For individuals beyond retirement the method runs into some difficulties although the logic of the method suggests that such individuals should most appropriately be valued at zero. (Depending on how it is applied, however, positive, negative or zero values are all possible.)

In some cases the measurement of lost output is taken net of consumption and in others a gross figure is used. The reasoning behind the adoption of a net of consumption estimate is that when an individual dies the rest of society loses the difference between what he would have produced and what he would have consumed. Which of these is correct—the gross or net figure—depends very much on the use which is to be made of the values. If the figures are to be used to provide some estimate of the loss involved in the death of an individual then the net of consumption figure is to be preferred. If the figures are to be used to indicate the benefits to be derived from saving someone from death then the gross figure is the relevant one. The difference is explained by the fact that in the former case the individual concerned is dead, is consequently no longer a member of society and therefore we can no longer talk of a loss to that individual who now no longer exists. In the latter case since we are approaching the problem from an *ex ante* standpoint, the individual involved is relevant because if his life is saved then he will continue to be a member of society, will continue to enjoy his consumption, and his consumption will therefore be part of the benefit to society (since he is a member of society). Consumption of the individual is therefore not deducted in this case. Given that the use to be made of the values is in valuing the benefits from investment in life-saving policies, the relevant figure to be used is the gross value. If, however, we wanted to estimate the loss to society from deaths in road accidents last year or the cost to the United States of the Vietnam War the relevant value would then be the net of consumption figure. (It is of interest to note that the basis of valuation of fatalities used by the Department of the Environment and the Transport Road Research Laboratory was changed from that of net of consumption to gross of consumption in 1971.)

56

5.3.2 *An Appraisal of the Approach*

What can we say in appraising this type of methodology? Its principal advantages are firstly that it is simple, secondly that wherever life has been valued up until very recently then this approach has been used and thirdly it is 'honest' in that its users have nearly always admitted that at best it is only measuring a part of the benefit of saving life. If the basic data on earnings, expectation of life, participation rates in the labour force, etc. are available then there are few problems thereafter in establishing actual values (although there may be a problem in determining the most appropriate rate at which to discount the benefits to reduce them to present value terms, of which more in appendix B). The main—and overriding—disadvantage of this 'human capital' approach is simply that it is not measuring that which we are interested in measuring, namely, the value of a reduction in risk of death or even the value of life. What it does measure, however, is livelihood.

Certainly if we were to accept that the sole goal of society was to maximise Gross National Product we might then be willing to adopt the 'human capital' value of life. Such a narrow goal is, however, unacceptable, although it is a goal which non-economists often attribute to economists (and not wholly because of misunderstandings on the part of the non-economists). The absurdity of the notion can perhaps best be exemplified by mentioning that it would lead at best to society refusing to raise a finger to aid elderly non-producers and at worst to a policy of killing off the old. Indeed this mistaken view has done more than any other factor to stifle debate on the question of what society should spend on life saving and it is only when economists cease to pursue these indefensible approaches that there is any prospect of policy-makers paying any attention to their ideas.

Furthermore, within its own terms of reference there is some difficulty in arguing that it is or could be claimed to be a way of providing even a minimum estimate of the value of life. The 'minimum value' argument rests on the premise that since the methodology measures accurately the labour aspect of life but leaves other aspects which also have a positive value unquantified, the human capital value is a lower limit estimate. However, given that we can learn nothing from the approach as to how much individuals would be prepared to pay to reduce their risk of death, we can only guess whether any 'true' value of life would be above or below the human capital value. (If we were to accept the imposed nature of the valuation process involved then of course we could argue that it represented a minimum value of what individuals *should* be prepared to pay. But given the problem remaining in determining the relationship between what individuals *would* be prepared to pay and what they *should* be prepared to pay this does not appear a useful avenue along which to proceed further.) The partial defence of the 'accounting' approach which has been mounted by Culyer and Akehurst[12], while having a certain academic appeal, is of little relevance to the broader debate of life valuation, once the concept of consumer sovereignty allied to risk reduction is accepted. But the essential point about the approach is that, other than the fact that we might expect a richer person to pay more than a poorer one to avoid death and a younger one more than an aged person, there seems no reason to think that there will be any relationship between what individuals are prepared to pay to avoid death and their future earnings.

Thus within a framework of cost-benefit analysis, based as it is on what individuals are or might be prepared to pay for some good or service, we would want so far as possible to determine the consumers' preferences for the good or goods under consideration. Any system of valuation which does not attempt to do this must inevitably result in 'imposed' values, the relationship between these and consumer preference-based values normally being unknown.

5.4 SOME CASE STUDIES OF THE HUMAN CAPITAL APPROACH TO LIFE VALUATION

5.4.1 *Dawson*

Dawson's[10,11] estimates of the costs of road accidents probably provide the best-known example in Britain of life valuation using the human capital approach. Dawson largely followed the precedent set by Reynolds[13]. He took the value of life as being measured in terms of lost output. Equating lost output with lost earnings for each age and sex group he estimated the value of future earnings allowing for participation rates in the work force and normal mortality. His basic argument was as follows

'When a worker (paid or unpaid) is prevented from working as a result of an injury, then in a time of full employment the community loses his production for the period of his incapacity. In the case of

58

death the position is more complicated, for whilst the community loses his future output it also saves his future consumption. The loss to the community is thus the difference between what would have been his future production and consumption, after both had been discounted to give present-day values'.

In the case of housewives' services, Dawson valued the output of housewives who did not go out to work at the average wage of employed women. For those who went out to work their output as housewives was valued at 50 per cent of the average wage rate of employed women.

To these estimates of the value of net output lost was added medical costs, to arrive at the 'economic' value of life. But Dawson went further than this. He states 'there are . . . other costs such as suffering and bereavement, that fall upon individuals. Although these are difficult to express in monetary terms their existence is very real to the persons concerned'. These costs Dawson calls the 'subjective costs'. He suggests a figure of £5000 as his estimate of the subjective cost of a fatal casualty. He argues: 'The use of subjective value of £5000 for a death means that when only paid output is valued the total average cost of a death is positive in all age and sex groups. £5000 is thus a minimum value; for if the community wishes to save the lives of persons although it would gain from their death, then the amount of gain which it foregoes is a minimum estimate of the value that is placed on keeping them alive'. He adds: 'A qualitative case could clearly be made for varying these costs according to the age of the victim, but it is not possible at present to do more than take average values'.

Thus the 'value of life' as estimated by Dawson in 1967 was £7880, £2880 of which was lost output and medical treatment, the remaining £5000 being the 'subjective' element. In his conclusions aside from differentiating between urban and rural areas in the valuation of fatalities Dawson did not differentiate between the values of different lives.

This 'net output' approach is quite common in the literature on valuation of life. However, by 1971 Dawson[11] was arguing in favour of a 'gross output' approach. His rationale for the change was that the use to be made of the values was primarily in the field of investment appraisal. Consequently whereas previously he had been concerned to estimate the losses to those remaining alive when an individual was killed (in other words, an *ex post* approach) he then argued that the valuation should be made *ex ante*. This meant in effect that the victim or potential victim was now considered to be a member of society and therefore to be part of the general economic calculus. What was required was to estimate the benefit to society including the potential victim of keeping him alive. Seen in this light the benefit is as before in terms of the costs saved to the rest of society but with the addition of the value of the consumption of the individual who has been saved. This is his future output gross and not net of his consumption.

5.4.2 *Rice and Cooper*

Rice and Cooper[14] adopt a similar approach to that of Dawson but without including the subjective costs. Their study measures only the value of life in terms of the present value of future earnings although the authors state that this is only one of the possible methods of measuring the value of human life. They say in their report that 'the value of a person is defined in terms of his economic worth as a productive member of society and the amount will vary according to age, sex, colour and degree of educational attainment'. They suggest that the presentation of data in this form will allow 'the economist to choose the most appropriate series of data for program evaluation'.

Of particular interest in this study are the differential values which emerge for different groups within society (in this case United States society). The two extremes they find are for a white man with 16 or more years of schooling, aged 30–34, who has a value of $223 471 and for a non-white man aged 85 and over with eight years of schooling who has a value of $596. Rice and Cooper imply therefore that the former life is equivalent to about 375 of the latter lives. If the lives considered are both male aged 30–34, the one white with 16 or more years of schooling and the other non-white with eight years of schooling, one life of the former category is equivalent to about three of the latter. No attempt is made to consider whether such differentiation of values in any way reflects the views of society nor whether such values would be acceptable to society. The only criterion for these particular authors is to provide 'the most appropriate series of data' for the *economist*. Viewed in their true light and without any attempt being made to make the values obtained by Rice and Cooper into something which they are not—namely values of life—the work of these authors is of course of value but as must by now be clear to

60

the reader they are of limited value, their limitations being emphasised by the equivalences between the lives outlined above. Even in the limited terms of their value as proposed by Rice and Cooper—providing data for the economist—given that the analysis yields what are in effect 'imposed' values, and no explicit account is taken of the preferences of the lives themselves, it is erroneous of them to suggest that an economist would accept these values as they stand in any analysis.

5.4.3 *Weisbrod*

Weisbrod[5] considers the methods of and prospects for quantification in the case of premature death. Using earnings as a proxy for the marginal product, he makes estimates of the potential loss of output arising as a result of premature death—allowing for a participation rate of 95 per cent in the labour force. Allowance is also made for the probability of an individual living from year to year, or expectation of life. Weisbrod considers the individual *ex post* and argues[5] (page 35) that 'in addition to involving the loss of a producer, a death also involves the loss of a consumer' and therefore deducts consumption from gross earnings. This net figure is then discounted through time. 'This' he states, 'is the value of a person as a net producer; it is the net value lost in the event of his death'. (The parallel to Dawson is very apparent.)

Weisbrod also makes allowance for housewives' services relating this to her 'market-orientated production' and her 'non-market, household production'. He makes the following interesting point[5] (page 40)

'An implicit assumption upon which the present value figures were constructed is that all cases of mortality from any disease are independent with respect to family—that is, occur in different families. If, in two different families, the husband in one and the wife in another were to die, the losses would be expected to be those we have computed. If, instead, the husband and wife in one family were to die, the total economic loss would be smaller; for example, if this were a two-person family there would be no need to replace the services of the housewife. The point is essentially this; much of the loss due to premature mortality is felt by the surviving family members; therefore, to the extent that there are no surviving family members, economic losses to all survivors are minimised'.

Weisbrod does consider the question of 'non-monetary costs'. He states[5] (page 96): 'The pain and anxiety felt by the sick person has been omitted because we have restricted our considerations to the losses *to others* of a person's poor health. The psychological burden carried by the victim's friends and relatives has been neglected simply because it seems to defy monetary measurement (at least for the present); but its omission . . . may not be critical'. This he argues on the basis that his primary objective is 'to illustrate a method of establishing priorities among health projects'. Thus although the grand total of losses may be understated, provided the relationship between quantified and unquantified losses is reasonably constant for different diseases, the emerging priorities will not be affected. He further argues that 'it is not improbable that the sentimental and psychological costs of poor health are roughly directly proportional to the number of cases and the number of deaths caused by the disease'. On the non-monetary costs of a disease and the age distribution of its victims, Weisbrod suggests that the 'sorrow' function associated with a death may be unimodal by age—being low in old age, comparatively low for very young children and peaking somewhere in between. He argues[5] (page 97) that whatever the reason for this 'what is significant is that the function would appear to be unimodal, and that this shape and the age-span at which it may reach a peak correspond roughly to the shape of the functions relating monetary costs of mortality to age'. From this he suggests that 'the covariation of non-economic with economic costs of mortality . . . adds plausibility to a contention that non-monetary costs are proportional to the monetary costs we have measured'.

Thus Weisbrod indicates that he is aware of the need to value housewives' services by imputing a certain economic output to them and his attempts to differentiate between housewives with differing degrees of 'burdens' is both intriguing and ambitious. More important, however, is his recognition of the need to do something about the 'non-economic losses' and while not disputing his proportionality point in theory, he perhaps ought to bring out more strongly the fact that he is restricting his view to the situation in which relative weights are the sole goal. But in the evidence Weisbrod presents on the possible relationship between monetary and non-monetary factors there is much that we would want clarified and validated before even begining to follow him along the particular path he would have us pursue.

62

5.4.4 *Klarman*

Klarman[8], in considering the benefits of a syphilis control programme, raises the problem of the measurement of consumer benefits from health programmes. He states

'A common difficulty in measurement is that few (if any) health services are pure investment goods or consumption goods that yield the same degree of health improvement. It is conventional to recognise the benefit in consumption derived from most health and medical care expenditures (such as reduction of pain, discomfort, etc.), to comment on the difficulties of measuring it, and then to dismiss it. What receives weight (and space) is what is measurable; and that is not necessarily important. Since the measurable segments—output loss and medical care expenditure—are not equally important in all programs being evaluated, their sum is not likely to bear a consistent relationship to the loss of the consumption benefit. Attaching a value to the latter, lest it be forgotten (or treated as zero), is both a sobering and challenging task'.

Klarman's approach to the problem of valuation is similar to that of Dawson in that there are two elements considered as benefit and dealt with wholly separately—the economic and 'non-economic' of Dawson and the investment and consumption goods of Klarman. Klarman goes on to pose the following: 'Suppose a person's lifetime income were guaranteed to him and his heirs, and health and medical services were furnished free of charge. Notwithstanding, would not many persons be willing to spend some money to avoid syphilis or to be cured of it in the early stages? It seems plausible to assume an affirmative answer. The question is, how much would they be willing to spend?'

In answer to this Klarman considers that one way of estimating the value of these consumption benefits for syphilis control is to relate the benefits to the costs of treating some other disease with similar symptoms but which treatment will not result in any benefit in the form of future earnings or a decrease in future medical expenditures. He considers for example that psoriasis (a skin disease) treatment costs give a reasonable proxy for the consumer benefits of treatment of syphilis cases in the infectious stages—about $50 per episode. For

63

cases of late complications of syphilis, he considers that 'an appropriate analogue is to be found in terminal cancer' giving an estimate of consumer benefit for such cases of about $2000 per case.

This line of Klarman's is certainly ingenious but it has limitations in that being based, for the consumption valuation, in the revealed preference approach any emergent values will tend to be lower limits (although this depends on the nature of the decision; see chapter 6). The approach also assumes that *already* the health services have been 'rationalised' to the extent that the amounts spent in different services are in some way a proxy for the benefits derived from the services *by the consumers*. While this is likely to be more true in the United States where there is something of a market for medical care (much more so than in Britain anyway) even there it is doubtful if the amount spent on treatment of psoriasis has a very close relationship to the benefit of the treatment to the individual. If it were the case that health services were bought like other services in the market place then this approach of Klarman's would have considerable merit. But given the fact that the market is very much insurance-covered there is little likelihood that the cost of treating terminal cancer has much connection with the consumption benefits to the consumer. Consequently the relationship between the costs of treating terminal cancer and the benefits *to the patient* of treating late complications of syphilis is likely to be rather remote. The relationship is likely to be even more remote under the British National Health Service. *But* if we relax our assumption that we wish to reflect consumers' preferences directly, Klarman's approach has more appeal—particularly in the context of socially implied values as discussed in the next chapter.

5.4.5 *Hanlon*

Hanlon[15] provides one of the most detailed accounts of the nature and significance of the 'human capital' type of approach. In doing so he compares man and machine directly: 'The human body may be considered as being similar to a machine. Like machines, its proper function depends on the movement and interaction of various physical and chemical parts, complicated and augmented, however, by a third and much more complex factor—biological reaction'. Hanlon recognises that the demand for such goods as health and life is a derived demand and that to talk of a direct demand for life is meaningless. He suggests in continuing his analogy with the machine

Table 5.1

Capital cost[i]	$
1 Economic incapacitation of mother	500
2 Risk of death to mother	12
3 Risk of injury to mother with immediate or subsequent effect on her economic value (prorated)	?
4 Immediate costs of child bearing	488
5 Risk of infant death (prorated)	40
6 Risk of infant illness or injury	?
7 Interest on capital investment	30
Total	1 070

Installation cost[ii]	
1 Shelter, clothing and food	11 900
2 Value of time mother devotes to child care	15 750
3 Education—family and community contribution	4 500
4 Medical and dental care and health protection	600
5 Recreation and transportation	3 000
6 Insurance	100
7 Sundries and incidentals	900
8 Risk of death during first 18 years (prorated)	250
9 Risk of disability during first eighteen years	?
10 Interest on installation costs	23 000
Total	60 000

Period of productivity[iii]	
Credit	
1 Earning potential	60 000
2 Interest on earnings	50 000
3 Non-economic potential	?
Total	110 000

Table 5.1—*continued*

Debit	$
1 Risk of disability during productive period	4 000
2 Medical costs	6 500
3 Risk of premature death	200
4 Risk of becoming substandard	5 500
5 Interest on debit items	15 000
Total	31 200

Notes

(i) The investment that society has in each infant by the time it is born.

(ii) The investment that society has in each individual by the time he reaches 18 years of age.

(iii) The return that society can expect from its investment, with the risks involved during this period.

that man has to be built, installed, maintained, etc. He then goes on to look at the 'items that contribute to the debit and credit columns of human life' and presents one such analysis although he stresses that it is intended solely as an illustration of the general principle which he is propounding. This example is of some interest to us and consequently his entries are summarised in table 5.1.

Having performed his calculations, Hanlon finds that 'there remains a net balance of about $18 000 per person for the individual's and society's provision for the period of obsolescence, retirement or senility'.

It has already been argued that this type of approach, exemplified here by Hanlon is not acceptable or at least that it leaves much to be desired. Such arguments need no repetition. However, if we were to ignore these objections to the particular type of methodology for the moment, even then there are some features of Hanlon's specific use of the method which need to be questioned. Firstly taking his capital cost items, these are all costs which fall on the parents or on a few occasions on the state acting *in loco parentis*. Now whereas it is relatively easy to agree with Hanlon that a machine has value only in so far as it produces, for example ballbearings, it is much more difficult to accept this as being true of a baby. But Hanlon states: 'If a man and a woman originally considered the pros and cons of prospective parenthood and, deciding against it, invested the total of the sums (on capital cost items) for a period corresponding to that of pregnancy, there would accrue at 3.5 per cent interest about $30. Although this may sound venal', he continues 'the fact remains that many people do just this'. Hanlon here is only concerned with 'interest on capital investment'—but what of capital investment itself? The $1040 on capital investment could have been spent on furniture for the house. If the mother and father decide that they would rather 'buy' baby than furniture then this would imply that they place a higher value on baby than on furniture. It also implies that the value of baby is at least equal to what they are prepared to pay as a 'purchase price'. Thus instead of there being a debit item for these costs it can be assumed that as far as the parents are concerned there is some non-negative credit item. Otherwise the child would not be 'purchased'. The same applies by and large to the installation costs if we could assume (as would be the case in less-developed societies) that such costs would all be met by the parents. Thus, as far as the parents are concerned we may liken the child more to a toy than to a machine for making ballbearings.

Once the child reaches the 'period of productivity' Hanlon is prepared to credit only post tax, post cost of living earnings and at the same time debit medical costs. Further, earnings are based on 'life expectancy' yet a debit entry is made for 'premature death'. If we make allowances for all these various points then we can recalculate Hanlon's sums as shown in table 5.2

Table 5.2

	$		$
Capital cost	1 070	Happiness to parents	1 070
Installation costs	60 000	Happiness to parents	60 000
Period of productivity			
Earning potential			60 000
Interest on earnings			50 000
Non-economic potential			?
Risk of disability	4 000		
Risk of being substandard	5 500		
Interest on debit items	10 000		
Total	80 570		171 070

The essential ingredient missing from Hanlon's analysis is the fact that men, unlike machines, think, feel, have attitudes and preferences, have children because they enjoy having children irrespective of their economic potential, etc. As Schelling[16] states: 'It is doubtful whether the interests of any consumers are represented in a calculation that treats a child like an unfinished building or some expensive goods in process' (and, we might add, like a ballbearing machine).

However Hanlon does say: 'The human mechanism differs from the mechanical contrivance in that it has abilities or potentials of incalculable value'. He asks: 'Who would dare appraise da Vinci, Beethoven, Shakespeare' and adds that 'the world is infinitely richer because of their existence'. Hanlon is thus prepared to pay lip service to some wider concept of the valuation of human life—but lip service only—as he pursues his much more restrictive valuation criteria.

But what of the implications of Hanlon's approach to the problem of valuing life generally? Should we take account of the costs imposed by the existence of an individual on the resources of society? Even if the general approach to life valuation can be improved ought account to be taken of some of Hanlon's debit items? The issue is complicated by the fact that in few of the fields in which resources are used for the capital costs, installation costs and debit items during the period of productivity, is there any general appraisal made of the benefits of such activities—education for example. Without knowing the basis of decision-making in such areas we are in something of a quandary to know whether or not we need to take account of Hanlon's debiting procedure.

But we are not here concerned with whether the present allocation of resources to and within, say, the education sector is optimal. All we can say is that this allocation is given and that for our purposes we must treat it as being optimal. Thus if any estimate were made of the benefits and costs of education (as has been done in academic circles and indeed to a limited extent in national policy circles) then some attempt would have to be made—or ought to be made—to incorporate mortality rates in such a way that the potential benefit for future years would reflect the demographic structure of society in future years. This would have to take account of the fatality rates from different sources—different diseases, road accidents, etc. depending on our particular interest. In so far as this procedure is followed then it would be incorrect to say that the death of a youth of 15 in a road accident was a loss in terms of the educational resources

68

he had used and a loss which should be 'borne' by road safety. The fact that the youth died at 15 should already be taken into account in the decision to allocate resources of a certain amount to education. If the youth is prevented from dying at the age of 15 then road safety contributes to the return on education, but the saving of the life and the increased benefits this saving brings is attributable wholly to the investment in road safety which prevented his death.

5.5 CONCLUSION

This chapter has indicated that there are very severe limitations on the value and usefulness of the concepts of human capital when applied to the problem of valuation of life—even though it has been the most commonly used method of valuation. First and foremost among the problems in using the approach there is the lack of a consumer preference base for valuation. This means in effect that the population at risk have little or no say in what values are placed upon their lives other than being assessed solely in terms of the size of their pay packets and their life expectancy. Despite the ingenuity shown by various writers to try to make the approach more acceptable one is left with the feeling that such efforts may well have been misdirected and might have been better channelled into a more basic search for a more fundamentally acceptable methodology of valuation.

REFERENCES

1. Schultz, T. W., Investment in human capital, *Amer. Econ. Rev.*, 1, March (1971)
2. Becker, G. S., Investment in human capital: a theoretical analysis, *J. Polit. Econ.*, Supplement, Oct. (1962)
3. Smith, A., *An Inquiry into the Nature and Causes of the Wealth of Nations*, Strahan and Cadell, London (1786)
4. Becker, G. S., *Human Capital, A Theoretical and Empirical Analysis with Special Reference to Education*, National Bureau of Economic Research, 121 and 122, New York (1964)
5. Weisbrod, B. A., *Economics of Public Health*, University of Pennsylvania Press, Philadelphia (1961)
6. Petty, Sir William, *Political Arithmetic or a Discourse Concerning the Extent and Value of Lands, People, Buildings, etc.*, Robert Clavel, London (1699)

7. Weisbrod, B. A., The valuation of human capital, *J. Polit. Econ.* 425, Oct. (1961)

8. Klarman, H. E., Syphilis control programs. In *Measuring Benefits of Government Investments*, ed. R. Dorfman, Brookings Institute, Washington, 367–414 (1965)

9. Dublin, L. I., and Lotka, A. J., *The Money Value of a Man*, Ronald Press, New York (1946)

10. Dawson, R. F. F., *Cost of Road Accidents in Great Britain*, Road Research Laboratory, Report LR 79 (1967)

11. Dawson, R. F. F., *Current Costs of Road Accidents in Great Britain*, Road Research Laboratory (1971)

12. Culyer, A. J., and Akehurst, R., On the economic surplus and the value of life, *Bull. Econ. Res.*, **26**, No. 2, 63–68, Nov. (1974)

13. Reynolds, D. J., The cost of road accidents, *J. Roy. Stat. Soc.*, **119**, 393–408 (1956)

14. Rice, D. P., and Cooper, B. S., The economic value of human life, *Amer. J. Public Health*, **57**, No. 11, 1954–1966, Nov. (1967)

15. Hanlon, J. J., *Principles of Public Health Administration*, C. V. Mosby, St. Louis, Chapter 7, 5th edn. (1969)

16. Schelling, T. C., The life you save may be your own. In *Problems in Public Expenditure Analysis*, ed. S. B. Chase, Brookings Institute, Washington (1968)

6

The Public Behavioural or Socially Implied Valuation Approach

6.1 AN OUTLINE OF THE APPROACH

6.1.1 *The Basic Rationale*

The second type of approach which has often been suggested as a means of improving decision-making in life-saving policy areas, is that of the 'public behavioural' or 'socially implied valuation' approach. The rationale behind this methodology can be stated quite simply. Given that there appear to be fundamental methodological problems in the 'human capital' approach to life valuation, it becomes necessary to look elsewhere for a solution to the problem. In so far as there appears no real prospect of improving on the methodology from the point of view of building in, in a theoretically acceptable manner, the element of consumers' preference which is missing from the accounting approach, a more pragmatic method needs to be found. One possibility is to examine the values implicit in decisions reached in the past on the allocation of resources to and the deployment of resources within life-saving areas. If a single value can be identified then it can in future be used explicitly throughout the whole of the public sector to aid decision-making in all areas concerned with life-saving. If a range emerges, then on a first assumption that all lives are equal, then we have a case for attempting to narrow the range of implied values.

In this way the problem of life valuation can be solved without recourse to elaborate or sophisticated economic models. This is achieved by taking the political process as the supreme arbiter. At the same time the across-the-board allocation to life-saving would in future be improved, in other words with a constant budget for life-

71

saving activities more lives would be saved in future then have been in the past. By adopting a single value of life throughout the public sector then more resources might be devoted to saving people from death in areas where the implied value is low and less in areas where the implied value of life is high. More people might then die as a result of, say, fire and fewer from, say, cancer, but overall the total lives saved would be increased.

If examination of implied values revealed a very wide dispersion then to take a mean or median value would be meaningless. None the less the areas which throw up the extremes in the range could be subject to fresh appraisal in the light of the knowledge that either too many or too few resources—depending on whether the values were at the top or bottom respectively of the range—were being devoted to these areas relative to the other areas being considered.

This approach is concerned with ensuring that, if a paternalistic attitude were to be adopted to such policy areas as health care and road safety then, in the interests of an efficient application of such paternalism, consistency should be sought in 'collective choice' decision-making. Given that the values would be determined by the political process and would thereby be 'imposed', there need be no relationship between the values emerging from this approach and those which would arise from a consumer sovereignty-orientated approach. This point serves to indicate yet again that there is no uniquely correct approach which is independent of the underlying political philosophy.

6.1.2 *The Underlying Conditions*

Harrison discusses the approach in the context of transport appraisal generally and suggests[1] that the following important conditions 'must hold if collective choices are to have force outside the immediate area of their application'. These are:

> 'First, the implications of the choices must have been correctly analysed and made clear to the decision-taker . . .
>
> second, either the choice must be simple or the choices frequent enough for analysis to be able to isolate the relevant factors with a sufficiently high degree of confidence . . .
>
> third, the analyst must be certain that the choices reflect genuine political preferences and not underlying administrative rules of thumb . . .

72

fourth, the effect must be sufficiently close in the areas concerned for the values to be transposed . . .

fifth, the choices must be reflections of current values . . .'

These are indeed formidable conditions. However, while Harrison is undoubtedly right to demand these for the values to emerge as wholly valid, the conditions can be relaxed and the calculation of the implied values still be of much use.

His first point is of course crucial for the implied values to be accepted as valid as they emerge. But part of our rationale for examining implied values is to determine why they depart either from some 'implied value norm' or from what the decision-makers meant to imply. If at the time of the decision the decision-maker did not fully understand the implications of the choice he faced then it may not only be the *value* that was implied, it may be that the *effects* were implied as well. If the decision-maker was unclear what the implications were but made some guess, then even if his guess were wrong it is that guess on which he made his decision—and it is valid to use this for obtaining the implied value.

Harrison's second point is unlikely to cause us too much concern in health care and road safety given the frequency if not always the simplicity of the choices involved. Similarly, his fifth point is no great obstacle in our chosen fields. His third point could certainly be problematical if decision-making in our two areas of concern were frequently subject to administrative rules of thumb. While it would be wrong to try to assert that health care and road safety decision-making were not afflicted in this way, such rules of thumb appear not to be so pervasive as to eliminate the prospects of unearthing sufficient choices reflecting 'genuine political preferences' to make the process viable. Finally, Harrison's fourth point can be overcome provided that an understanding is acquired at the same time as the series of implied vlaues, as to what factors influence the level of the implied values. If for example differentials in implied values can largely be explained in terms of, say, life expectation of those saved and the initial level of risk, then there seems no reason why values can not be transposed from one area such as risk of drowning to another very different area such as road safety.

It may of course be unduly optimistic to assume away some of the problems which Harrison implies. Some of the conditions if they do not hold initially will perhaps be more likely to hold by the pursuit of the process itself. For example, the presentation to the decision-makers of the information that the vlaue of life implied by a particular decision was £10 million might make them appreciate that they need to be much more explicit about their decision-making processes and perhaps *not* be content to rely on rules of thumb or not be unclear about the implications of their choices. This tedious process may be some distance removed from that of obtaining valid and viable implied values reflecting Harrison's full conditions, but pressing ahead with the process may in itself help to bring about the conditions.

6.1.3 *Use and Benefits of the Approach*

To embark on an exercise to elicit the values implied in various past decisions would undoubtedly prove of considerable value. Indeed studies are reported below which have attempted to estimate implied values in some areas although not in as comprehensive a manner as is ideally required. There is little doubt that such an approach could result in a more consistent—and hence presumably better—allocation of resources to life-saving activities in the public sector. An examination of some implied values in various fields reveals immediately that there is a very wide range of implied values of life not only as between different sectors but also within the same sector. For example, following Ronan Point, as a result of the partial collapse of this block of high-rise flats and the resulting deaths, various changes were made to the building regulations. According to the calculations of Sinclair *et al.*[2] the total cost of these together with the estimated resultant reduction in risk, implied a minimum valuation of life of more than £20 million. On the other hand it has been claimed in one investigation[3] that a method of preventing stillbirths could be standard practice for a cost of approximately £50 per life saved. Since this was not widely used at the time it tends to suggest that in this case we can treat the £50 as a maximum value, giving us a total range of less than £50 to greater than £20 million per life saved.

Without seeking to cast any doubts on the methods used in calculating these figures, it is worth emphasising that these figures are best considered as orders of magnitude rather than precise estimates. This follows directly from the difficulties which exist in all such studies in attempting to ensure that the assumptions used are accurate. This is frequently an almost impossible task because it involves a close reconstruction of the actual evidence and decision process involved at the time the decision was taken.

74

Nevertheless we have here at least prima facie grounds for thinking that there is some misallocation of resources to life-saving activities. The examples also serve to indicate the difficulty in comparing lives saved—in this instance 'innocent families in the sanctity of their homes' and 'unborn babes'.

6.1.4 *The Non-homogeneity of Lives*

The issue of the non-homogeneity of lives saved is not peculiar to the public behavioural approach. It was touched on briefly in chapter 1 but since it is of particular relevance to the approach discussion in this chapter, some more detailed account of the point is required. To define the outputs of different life-saving programmes in terms of a supposed common unit of 'lives saved' may be unrealistic. There are various reasons why we might expect 'lives saved' in one area to be different from 'lives saved' in another. For example, the output of a cervical cancer screening programme is likely to be in terms of lives saved among middle aged multiparous women of lower socioeconomic classes whereas the Tufty Clubs, the National Cycling Proficiency Scheme and the Green Cross Code are only likely to affect children on the roads. The 'quality of life' on a kidney machine is likely to be very much lower than that of individuals saved from drowning. The future expectations of life of lives saved through the provision of coronary care units will differ markedly from that of lives saved through child-proof containers for medical prescriptions. Attitudes to death may vary according to circumstances—death from cancer may be thought more abhorrent (and consequently of greater value when avoided) than death in a road accident which is frequently instantaneous; the prospect of accidental death 'at home' (Ronan Point, for example) may give rise to greater anxiety than that of death in an accident at work (construction workers, for example); and again the lone yachtsman stranded in mid-Atlantic is in a very different situation to that of the average family motorist going for a week-end jaunt in the British countryside. It follows from this that it could be 'rational' to have different implied values emerging in different circumstances. However, without some empirical research it is difficult to judge the extent of differentials likely to emerge.

What we can do, as a first step, is to try to reach agreement on the relevant factors which might lead to such differentials and the direction of the differentials. Table 6.1 represents one view of some of

Table 6.1

Factor	Value above 'mean public sector value'	Value below 'mean public sector value'
Age	Young	Old
Family circumstances	(for example) married man with young family	(for example) single male with no dependants
Nature of threat to life	(for example) cancer	(for example) instantaneous death in road accident
Future expectation of life	long	short
Quality of future life	normal	below average
Level of risk	high	low
'Fairness' of risk	'external'—unable to be influenced by individual	'internal'—self-imposed
Absolute change in risk	small	large
Circumstances of risk	(for example) at home	(for example) driving

the relevant factors and whether they might result in lower or higher values.

Thus this issue of 'non-homogeneity' of lives saved means that we would not expect a single public sector value to emerge. At the same time it follows that any further research in this area would need not only to identify the implied values but also to provide a detailed description of the lives saved and the circumstances of the reduced mortality. The table above represents only a first attempt at listing relevant factors. A more comprehensive discussion of what factors are relevant is required as a precursor to the more arduous task of determining the extent of the differentials appropriate for different factors. The general point however can be made that in applying values, whether derived from the public behavioural approach or not, we need to be careful that they are appropriate for the use being made of them.

6.1.5 *Problems of Minimum, Maximum, Average and Marginal Values*

A further difficulty arises from the fact that where policies have been implemented the implied values of life which emerge will normally be minimum or maximum values. This is true where a decision is a 'yes' or 'no' one rather than a 'how much' one. With the former type of decision all we would probably know would be that the decision-makers were prepared to devote *at least* some known amount of resources to the policy but we might well not know anything about the maximum sum which they would be prepared to pay for it. Frequently all we can hope to know is that the decision was implemented at a known level of expenditure and this allows us to say that the decision-makers involved must have implicitly considered that they were prepared to spend *at least* that sum on the policy. There is no way in such circumstances of moving from this minimum value to the mean or any other.

In some cases however we will be better placed. For example it may be that a series of incremental policies was considered, each involving the use of more and more resources but with diminishing returns with respect to the number of lives saved. This would mean that the cost of saving the marginal life was increasing. In such instances it may be possible to obtain either a more or less accurate estimate of the implicit value of life or at least a lower and upper limit to the range within which it must lie. This would follow if in the circumstances described the chosen option fell short of saving the highest number of lives possible, the implicit rationale being that at that level of low risk the expenditure involved to achieve it was not 'justified'. (See for example the cervical cancer case quoted in chapter 4, section 4.2.) The extent to which this aspect of the approach could prove to limit its value is obviously dependent upon the extent to which we are blessed with a surfeit of 'incremental' type decisions in life-saving policy-making and the extent to which we are cursed with the 'yes'/'no' type of decision.

6.1.6 *Data Problems*

At a more fundamental level one of the problems associated with this 'public behavioural' approach is that there are in practice comparatively few areas of policy-making where the necessary detail is available on the effectiveness of different policies to allow estimates to

77

be made of the value of life embodied in particular decisions. Often decisions will have been taken without very much quantitative information. The basis of decision-making may have been qualitative in essence. In such cases it may not be possible to estimate what the trade-off is between resources used and lives saved. Again, of course, as the discussion in the previous paragraph indicated, ideally what is required is to establish the implied value at the margin, but data availability—aside from the problem of 'yes'/'no' decisions—may well hamper such research.

The other difficulty in this area is that of the joint benefits arising from a particular policy. It will often be the case that the benefits of a particular project will extend beyond those of simply life saving; reductions in morbidity and injury may well be present as may certain material benefits such as savings in damage costs to vehicles with the operation of some road safety policies. Fire prevention is another case in point. Where this kind of situation occurs it may be possible to disentangle the life element in which lies our prime interest but in many cases this will not be feasible.

6.2 SOME APPLICATIONS

6.2.1 Tractor Cabs

Sinclair[4] discusses legislation introduced in Britain to make the fitting of cabs to farm tractors compulsory. He writes: 'About 100 000 tractors are produced for the home market each year. Because each has an average life of five years, all the 500 000 British farm tractors will be equipped with cabs by 1974. Roughly 40 lives a year will have been saved at an annual cost of £40 for a frame per cab, borne directly by the farming community'. This is almost a classic case of 'implied life values' in public decision-making, in this instance stated in the legal framework of standards. At a total cost of £20 million over five years, 200 lives will be saved thus implying that a minimum value of life for a tractor driver is about £100 000. Other benefits will be obtained in terms of reduced exposure to the elements, thereby making a tractor driver's lot a happier one and possibly also saving a number of working days previously lost through illness. In so far as these benefits were considered relevant in reaching the decision to legislate, then the implied value of life figure would be reduced below the £100 000 figure estimated above. It should be noted however that the mere existence of these other benefits is not sufficient to reduce the

78

implied value of life figure; it is only in so far as they were considered relevant to the decision that we need to take account of them.

While without further knowledge of the decision environment it is not possible to say whether any other options were considered, this particular decision appears very much as a simple 'do' or 'don't' case. By deciding to legislate (and assuming that the other benefits were not considered relevant) the only value we can draw from this example is that of a minimum value. Had the decision gone the other way and nothing been done then a maximum value would have been implied (again of £100 000). Nor can anything be said of marginal values without more information.

6.2.2 *Hine on Health*

Hine[5] has made an investiagation into the implied values of life which emerge from a study of health care policies in the treatment of certain types of conditions and diseases. He acknowledges the fact that in the health field it is frequently difficult to establish the effectiveness of health care regimes, knowledge which is required before any estimate of implied values of life can be made. Hine gives various reasons for this, for example, the problem of medial ethics which means that once it is established that a particular practice yields some health benefits it then becomes ethically impossible to mount randomised control trials to establish just how effective the treatment is; populations treated will not necessarily be homogeneous; and practices vary from region to region and from hospital to hospital.

In his case study on renal dialysis Hine concludes: 'On average cost of treatment for all patients that first receive dialysis is £14 000 for eight years of life or £1666 per year of life'. Given that only one-eighth (according to Hine) of persons who could benefit from dialysis do in fact get this treatment he concludes that 'a minimum value of life for one-eighth of those who can benefit from dialysis is a value of £1666 per year'. For a mobile coronary care unit Hine estimates a total cost of £1079 per life saved for an expectation of life of about five years—averaging £216 per year of life saved. In screening for cervical cancer Hine gives a figure of about £2000 per life saved, which given an expectation of life of ten years is equivalent to about £200 per year of life saved. In the case of lung cancer X-rays for old smokers Hine estimates a cost of £420 for five years of life, £84 per year of life saved; for heart transplant an initial cost of £3000 and thereafter a cost of £200 per year lived; and for kidney transplant an initial cost of £1000 and thereafter an annual cost of £200.

Before leaving Hine it is worth emphasising that in this 'public behavioural' approach exemplified by Hine's examination of new forms of treatment in the field of health, despite the element of homogeneity introduced by Hine's restriction of his area of concern to that of health, what emerges is (perhaps we should add not surprisingly) that we have not only a fairly wide 'spread' of minimum values but also a fairly wide 'spread' of lives involved and of quality of life enjoyed. The middle-aged dialysis patient is obviously not directly comparable with the embryonic baby not only in terms of their life situations prior to treatment but also in terms of their qualities of life after or in the course of treatment. The baby may be restored to complete normality. The dialysis patient on the other hand is quite likely to become mentally ill because of his complete dependence on the machine. He will also have a restricted style of life both in terms of physical effort and socially for a comparatively short future. This problem is not meant in any way as criticism of Hine's application of the approach. It simply serves to highlight the nature of the problem involved in attempting to value lives which are frequently not homogeneous.

6.2.3 *The Lone Yachtsman*

A further example of the public behavioural approach is that of the resources which society is prepared to devote to the saving of the lives of individuals who are in particularly perilous situations, such as where they face a risk of death which, unless some effective action is taken, will approximate to unity. Examples of this are lone yachtsmen stranded in the Atlantic, climbers lost in the mountains, and potholers who have got themselves trapped. Such cases tend to make front page news with much detailed commentary on the rescue operations which have been put in hand to save the unfortunate individuals. It could be argued from this that if society is prepared to devote hundreds of thousands of pounds to save an individual in such circumstances then this provides some estimate of the minimum value of life. If the value were less than this then presumably the resources would not be expended.

The usefulness of this type of approach is very limited, for three main reasons. Firstly, the type of situation involved here is very different from the run-of-the-mill small reduction in small-risk types of situations which are common to life-saving policies in the public sector. Without the intervention of some other party the stranded lone yachtsman will almost certainly die. There is really no parallel in road safety where the individuals with whom we are concerned are faced with a very low probability of death on any equivalent trip. Again in health care while individual medical practitioners may be faced with rather similar situations from time to time, in terms of planning the allocation of health resources, 'certain death' situations involving identifiable individuals are very rare indeed.

Secondly, the individuals are readily identifiable. Even if, prior to their being reported lost, they are unknown, they quickly become famous through the mass media as James Conroy with a wife and three young children living in a semidetached in Orpington, where the wife is interviewed and describes the aspirations and driving force behind the husband who has landed himself in his present predicament. It is very difficult to connect this type of individual with the approximately 15 million drivers who each day place themselves at risk at a very low level and who only become identified after the event which results in the deaths of a handful of them.

Thirdly, the fact that the number at risk in the two situations are so very different makes the relationship between the two even more remote. It can be argued that it is largely because there are so many individuals at risk and so many deaths and injuries on the road that the government 'interferes' and regulates the use of the roads. Were it the case that over 7000 individuals were dying in 'lone yachts' in the Atlantic each year—and presumably therefore many more placing themselves in such potentially risky situations—it is extremely unlikely that first of all the government would *not* step in to regulate the activity and secondly that public opinion would look as favourably on the rescue operations involved when it became apparent just how great a problem this had become and the cost to the exchequer of dealing with it.

As with other areas of 'public behavioural' implied values it would of course be interesting to investigate the costs involved in rescue operations of this type and also to determine what factors are involved in deciding when to call off a search. (One would imagine that virtually the sole criterion for the latter is the judgment that the probability that the individual concerned is still alive is so small as to be negligible but it is possible that some element of the incremental cost of continuing the operation may creep in.)

81

The type of risk involved in these cases is by and large the voluntary risk which Mishan describes[6]. If Mishan is right in assuming that where risk is voluntarily assumed then we need not concern ourselves with it in any cost-benefit framework—since it will be already built in to the demand for such activities as rowing singlehanded across the Atlantic—would he therefore draw the conclusion that we ought not to spend resources on saving such persons? Alternatively Mishan might argue that were potential rowers across the Atlantic aware of the fact that should they get into difficulties then society would not take any action to save them, the scale of such activities would be decreased. In other words, it could be argued that the demand for such activities is 'artificially' high because of the 'subsidisation' of the risk-bearing cost component. While this argument may well be valid in theory it is difficult to believe that the threat of no action to save a stranded yachtsman could or ever would be carried out in practice.

6.2.4 *Life-long Support*

Another approach under the general head of public behavioural implied values is that which states that in our society an individual who is born with some deficiency which results in his being totally unable to support himself and being wholly dependent on the community (or the State) will be provided for by that community or State. For example an orphaned thalidomide child would be cared for by the State and certainly not left to perish. If we could estimate the total life-long cost of caring for such an individual then we would have an estimate of what society was *at least* prepared to pay to 'save' a life.

What is immediately striking about this approach is how atypical it is of the type of situation with which we are normally concerned in public sector decision-making. It is in effect a rather similar type of case to the lone yachtsman although in some respects even more extreme. Where this type of situation does become of more relevance within our specific field of interest is when choices have to be made on whether or not to let a new-born baby live or die. It would appear for example that some children born with spina bifida are allowed to die shortly after birth. To suggest that this policy was based on the financial cost of caring for them would be distasteful at the very least. Nonetheless not acting positively to encourage some such children to live is a recognition that even when dealing with specific identifiable lives there are limits beyond which society is not willing to go to retain the sanctity of human life. This is particularly true when it is appreciated that the 'life' involved is likely to be a difficult one and maintained at a very high cost in terms not just of finance but also of the suffering of the victim and his relations and friends. This apart, however, this form of social valuation of life is perhaps the most inappropriate of all and need not concern us further. There is little if anything to be gained from a study of these 'life-long' costs. Undoubtedly society will continue to support most of such cases and it would be totally false to argue that this was in some way wrong.

6.2.5 *Court Awards*

The case of court awards is a form of publicly implied valuation although somewhat different from the examples quoted thus far. In so far as the courts are required to assess the amount of damages to be paid to victims killed or injured in certain circumstances the amounts paid might be expected to reflect the values which society as a whole might wish to place on such compensation. A study of awards for damages in the case of fatalities might be one way of establishing the value of life to be used in decision-making.

Before considering this proposal it is necessary to outline how and in what circumstances these awards are made and how the sums are calculated. (Methods of compensation vary considerably from one country to another; what is said here relates to Britain.) Compensation is paid on the grounds—almost solely—of the tort of negligence. There are three basic requirements which must be met in such cases. Firstly, the defendant must owe a 'duty of care' to the plaintiff. This allows judges to exclude claims from certain persons by indicating that the relationship with the defendant was not sufficiently close for the plaintiff to warrant benefit from the tort of negligence. Secondly, for negligence to be proved it must be shown that the defendant's conduct was below the standard that it would be reasonable to expect from a normal person in the circumstances involved. This is a flexible standard which allows the judges some discretion. Thirdly, it has to be proved that it was the negligence of the defendant which did in fact result in the injury occurring. (For a more detailed account see Harris[7].)

Thus before considering what damages should be paid, the court must be satisfied that all three requirements are met. In theory each individual case is considered on its own merits. However there is in effect an 'unofficial scale of compensation' which has been built up through previous judgments. (This is based on reports of awards made in the monthly journal *Current Law*.)

In general the sum paid by way of compensation is a single sum covering 'general damages' and the various component parts are seldom valued separately. These component parts cover pain and suffering, both past and future; loss of amenities (disfigurement, for example); loss of expectation of life (for which a relatively fixed sum of £500 is normally given); and loss of expected earnings. In the case of a fatal accident 'compensation is assessed on the basis of the number of years during which the widow and children expected to be financially dependent on the earnings of the deceased, and this in turn depends on the number of future 'earning' years which the deceased could have expected just before the accident'[7]. This is generally reduced to allow for 'contingencies of life', such as the fact that the individual killed might not have been in employment throughout the rest of his expected working life.

There are various reasons why judges may reduce the assessment of damages. Firstly, if the plaintiff is held to be partly to blame, then the damages given will be reduced by a proportion equivalent to the proportion of blame resting with the plaintiff. (In the Oxford study[8] one-quarter of those who received damages through the tort of negligence had their assessment of damages reduced in this way.) Secondly, all taxes and social security payments are deducted and thus the sum paid is net of such taxes. Thirdly, a deduction is made of one half of any sums paid by way of industrial injury benefit, disablement benefit or sickness benefit or any such sums the plaintiff is likely to receive in the next five years. Fourthly, if an employer continues to pay his employee during the period he is absent from work due to his injuries, this sum is also deducted. In the case of a death, relatives may claim for damages but only for the balance of pecuniary losses sustained by them. The court may give only such damages as it may think proportionate to the pecuniary loss of the relations by reasons of the death of the injured person. The effect is that the relations can only recover compensation for the actual pecuniary loss sustained by them, and the sufferings of the deceased or the mental pain occasioned to the relatives of the loss of companionship (in the case of a husband or wife) cannot be taken into account by the jury when assessing the damages. However, it is possible for the administrators of the deceased's estate to pursue a separate action for loss of the deceased's earnings, expenses and suffering in the period between the accident and death. If the relatives gain from this claim, the total amount by which they gain is deducted from the damages they receive through their own claim.

It is of interest to note that under Scots Law compensation until recently could be paid for the suffering of the deceased's relatives under the heading of 'solatium' (see Gloag and Henderson[9]). Under the Damages (Scotland) Act 1976 this 'solatium' award has been replaced by a 'loss of society' award which is defined as 'compensation for loss of the benefit of the society of the deceased, and the guidance that would have been provided by the deceased if he or she had not died' (see *Journal of the Law Society of Scotland*[10]).

A further difficulty in using court awards for valuation purposes is that they represent only the tip of the iceberg of compensation paid. For example the Harris and Hartz study[8] found that in a survey of 90 seriously injured persons only 58 per cent made claims for damages, and only 42 per cent of the total were successful in obtaining damages. These figures do not include any cases of fatalities but they do suggest that there may well be serious shortcomings in the way in which the law operates in this area of compensation and/or that there is considerable ignorance on the part of victims as to their rights with respect to making claims for compensation. Ison does, however, suggest[11] that 'There is some evidence that the larger the claim the more likely it is to be fought up to judgment'.

From the above it is apparent that to use court awards as implied social values for life, limb or disability would be very much an imperfect solution. Those cases which get to the courts and which result in damages being awarded are certainly not a representative sample. This difficulty could of course be overcome by a study of all awards made whether in or out of court. However there are more serious drawbacks to the court awards method. Principal among these is the fact that the awards are made *ex post*. Further, in so far as any allowance is made for pain and suffering the amount paid is very low, virtually a nominal sum. Indeed what court awards tend to indicate is the financial dependency of the deceased's relatives on the deceased. Economists could undoubtedly provide a more accurate assessment of this than judges and if it were this aspect of life valuation in which we were interested we need go nowhere near the courts to obtain our values. We would in effect settle for the human capital approach of chapter 5.

6.3 CONCLUSION

While this type of approach has a very definite pragmatic appeal to it, there is a danger that unless it is considered in full awareness of its restricted application it could conceivably result in new anomalies being created. Indeed there is, beyond the virtue of consistency—and it is a virtue that has to be qualified—a certain fatalistic 'vicious circle' ring to the method. In the areas in which government is concerned with the saving of life we must doubt whether the basis for decision-making is sufficiently rational to allow that anything like consistent values will emerge. But not only this; there is little reason to believe that the decisions being made which imply values close to some mean or median value are in any sense more correct than values emerging at the extremes of the range. While there is undoubtedly some merit in a methodology which might result in more lives being saved from the same expenditure, the methodology may indicate little more than that decision-making in this area of life saving is not an exact science. What the method may reveal—and in gaining acceptance for valuing human life it may in the long run be no small benefit—is the extent of this inexactitude.

However, it can be argued that the government does attempt to reflect the views, preferences and wishes of the public. This partial reflection of consumer sovereignty implies acceptance at the same time of the value judgment on which the concept of using cost-benefit analysis in the valuation of the public sector projects is based. On this basis the 'public behavioural' approach has a distinct advantage over the 'accounting' approach. Consequently it is suggested that there is merit in pursuing the method, albeit in full recognition of its limitations.

As indicated by the case studies quoted in this chapter some work has already been conducted on implied values. However, this type of work is generally very poorly researched and there is a genuine need for more extensive work to be done.

The fact that it tends to have us chasing our tails in that the existing values will tend to be endorsed (whether they are in any sense right or not); that there are good reasons for expecting the values to differ for various reasons and not to be based on a single value of life in the whole of the public sector; that there are severe practical difficulties involved in deriving the implicit values at the margin and in sufficient different situations; all these would have us question how much value to attach to this approach. It can provide a mechanism whereby the standard of decision-making in areas of activity concerned with life saving could be improved and made more rational than at present. It could allow more lives to be saved under the existing ceiling of expenditure on life saving than is currently the case. While this may not result in an optimum allocation of resources within the life-saving field it will certainly result in an increase in welfare of society as a whole—and that is judged to be a sufficient justification.

REFERENCES

1. Harrison, A. J., *The Economics of Transport Appraisal*, Croom Helm, London (1974)
2. Sinclair, T. C., Marstrand, P., and Newick, P., *Human Life and Safety in Relation to Technical Change*, Science Policy Research Unit, University of Sussex, April (1972)
3. Heys, R. F., Oakey, R. E., Scott, J. S., and Stitch, S. R., Practicability and cost of oestriol assays for saving babies in a maternity hospital, *Lancet*, 331–332, Feb. 17th (1968)
4. Sinclair, T. C., Costing the hazards of technology, *New Scientist*, Oct. 16th (1969)
5. Hine, J. L., *M.A. Dissertation*, (unpublished), University of Leeds (1971)
6. Mishan, E. J., *Cost Benefit Analysis*, George Allen and Unwin, London, chapters 22 and 23 (1971)
7. Harris, D. R., *Analysis of the British Auto-Accident Compensation System, in Comparative Studies in Automobile Accident Compensation*, US Department of Transportation Automobile Insurance and Compensation Study, April (1970)
8. Harris, D. R., and Hartz, S. J., A road accident survey, *New Law J.*, 492 (1969)
9. Gloag, W. M., and Henderson, R. C., *Introduction to the Law of Scotland*, W. Green and Son, Edinburgh, 7th edn. (1968)
10. *J. Law Soc. Scot.*, June (1976)
11. Ison, T. G., *The Forensic Lottery*, Staples Press, London (1967)

7

The Preferred Valuation Methodology: The Valuation of Reduction in Risk of Death

7.1 INTRODUCTION

It is perhaps worth emphasising at the beginning of this chapter that there is no apparent readily available ideal solution to the problem of valuation of human life. There are grounds for believing however, as previous chapters have already indicated, that some (but not all) of those efforts which have been made in the past to value life have been somewhat misconceived. This has increased the difficulties in attempting to take economics into this field and to use it to improve decision-making in life-saving activities. There is no single method which will immediately allow benefits of reductions in mortality to be measured in a wholly satisfactory way. None the less it is possible to outline the type of approach which is likely to lead us along the right path—even although we must for the moment consider the approach principally from a conceptual and theoretical point of view and record some doubts as to its applicability in practice. While this is not wholly satisfactory, it does mean that we can at least narrow the field of possible methods to the one which appears most likely to be acceptable.

This chapter introduces the method and reviews its comparatively short history. In the chapters which follow the method is considered in more detail and various implications of its possible use in practice are spelt out.

7.2 THE METHODOLOGY

7.2.1 *The Background to the Methodology*

Drèze[1] appears to have been the first to consider in any detail the question of life valuation along the lines which could be classified as being soundly based in the principles of cost-benefit analysis and consumer sovereignty. He suggested that the cost incurred by an individual to avoid a particular risk of premature death might be freely determined by that individual and consequently the utility of his life would freely reflect his scale of preferences and values. He first considered that the cost or amount paid might well vary depending on the size of the risk and the nature of the risk and also on such circumstances as pension and insurance benefits.

Later Schelling[2] in the very title of his essay—'The life you save may be your own'—emphasised the need to bring the potential victims into the picture. He started: 'Is death so awesome, so frightening, and so remote, that in discussing its economics we must always suppose that it is someone *else* who dies?' He saw the question of valuation in terms of life saving rather than life itself thereby making the important switch in emphasis from the 'investment in man' approach to posing the question 'what is it worth to reduce the probability of death—the statistical frequency of death—within some identifiable group of people none of whom expects to die except eventually?'

Schelling also considered why it is that the treatment of the valuation of life has to be different from that used to value other goods or other benefits in a cost-benefit framework. He claimed

'What makes a barn or shop easier to evaluate than a life ... is that it is less difficult to guess what it is worth to the man who owns it. Its replacement cost sets an upper limit. Even that, though, does not directly tell the worth of a small increment in a small probability of material destruction; it is the insurability of the structure, with a policy that pays off in the same currency with which one buys replacement, that makes it possible to estimate the worth to a man of an incremental change in the risk of fire, collision or windstorm'.

While others can insure against the loss of the individual concerned—at least in terms of the financial loss—the individual himself cannot insure himself for the loss of his own life. As Schelling said: 'This is what is not insurable in terms that permit replacement. This is the consumer interest in a unique and irreplaceable good'.

This, however, is not the whole difference in explaining the need to use a different type of methodology in valuing lives from that used for the value of, barns, for instance. Part of the explanation lies in the fact that there is in the case of risk of death as compared with the risk of loss of some other more normal 'good' a very much stronger component which is based on fear, anxiety or some other such 'psychic' loss—the nomenclature is irrelevant. It may well be that fear is also present in the case of the barn owner but the difference in degree is so marked as to constitute a difference in substance. (The anxiety point is considered in much more detail in chapter 8.)

All other things being equal the individual who owns an insured barn (assuming his insurance covers not only the cost of replacing the barn but also meets any inconvenience or other costs arising if it is destroyed) will be indifferent as to whether his barn burns down or not. He therefore has no cause for alarm or anxiety regarding the future existence or non-existence of his barn. It is this non-insurability, irreplaceability, anxiety-linked feature of the good 'life' which separates it from other goods when we come to evaluate it. Those who have argued that it is a nonsense to attempt to place a value on life because there is no 'market' for life have drawn the wrong conclusion from what is almost a correct premise. What can be said is that since there is no market for life *for the life in question* a departure from the normal type of methodology used for valuation of goods and services is required. It is this type of feature to which Zeckhauser[3] refers when he suggests that there is no comprehensive contingent claims market for his 'probabilistic individual preferences' (PIP) goods, and he would almost certainly accept along with Schelling that in the case of the option of life saving or the PIP good of reduction of risk of death there is no contingent claims market at all as far as the individual at risk is concerned. (Zeckhauser's 'PIP' goods are discussed in more detail in chapter 8, section 8.2.2.) It is largely for this reason that values of life emerging from life insurance data are not of much use to us in attempting to place a value on life (see section 7.5 below). This point is made by Bailey[4] when commenting on Schelling: 'The term insurance policy removes the financial risk associated with the hazard without removing the personal risk, whereas the safety program does both. A safety program is an insurance policy that also keeps the man in the picture'.

Thus in switching the emphasis to life *saving* we are attempting to 'keep the man in the picture' and take his opinions, values and views into account. We are not concerned with what the effect would be as a result of an individual's death because to see the problem in these terms immediately infers that we are not concerned with the victim or individual at risk himself. Since we are eventually looking to improve decision-making in the field of life saving and as a result use resources in this field in such a way as to save more lives we are compelled to take the views of the whole of society into account and not just the survivors in the *ex post* situation.

7.2.2 *Jones-Lee's Theoretical Contribution*

Jones-Lee[5-7] has pursued in greater detail this suggestion of Schelling's that we ought to adopt a methodology of evaluation based on valuing reductions in risk of death. Indeed his contributions at a theoretical level (and also at an applied level—see 7.5.5 below) are central to the theme of this book.

He suggests[7] that 'we must inquire—first at the individual level and then at the aggregate level—into the relationship between the magnitude of a decrease in risk and the maximum amount that would be paid to affect that change'. He thus claims that 'the problem is clearly one of choice under uncertainty' and in developing his theme he draws on the literature on choice under uncertainty, and in particular the work of Hirshleifer[8], Ramsey[9], Savage[10], Shackle[11] and von Neumann and Morgenstern[12].

Now if it is assumed that an individual prefers a low probability of death to a high probability (in other words, there is a disutility associated with death and consequently any positive risk of death—see appendix A for a discussion of attitudes to death) then we can assume that the individual would be prepared to forfeit some of his present wealth to effect a reduction in the probability of death in the same period.

Thus if the individual starts the period with wealth $\bar{w}$ and his own assessment of his likelihood of death (that is, the subjective probability) is $\bar{p}$, then his initial expected utility is given by

$$E(U) = (1 - \bar{p})L(\bar{w}) + \bar{p}D(\bar{w})$$

where $L(\bar{w})$ is the utility of wealth function conditional on survival during the period and $D(\bar{w})$ is the utility function conditional on death during the period.

91

Jones-Lee then supposes 'that the individual is offered the opportunity to reduce the probability of his death during the current period from $\bar{p}$ to $p(<\bar{p})$'. The individual will be prepared to give up as a maximum, that sum, v 'such as to leave him with the same level of expected utility as in the initial situation'. The value of v can then be obtained from the following:

$$(1-p)L(\bar{w}-v) + pD(\bar{w}-v) = (1-\bar{p})L(\bar{w}) + \bar{p}D(\bar{w})$$

in other words the utility of being alive at the end of the period having forfeited v, multiplied by the increased probability of living plus the utility of being dead at the end of the period having forfeited v, multiplied by the reduced probability of dying during the period, is equal to the utility of being alive at the end of the period multiplied by the original probability of living plus the utility of being dead at the end of the period multiplied by the original probability of dying.

For this simplest case of a single time period in which the individual is not insured, Jones-Lee examines three aspects of the relationships between p, the risk of death and v, the maximum sum the individual would be prepared to forfeit to reduce his risk or the minimum sum he would be willing to accept to have his probability of death increased. From the general form of the relationship he establishes that

(1) the individual will not be prepared to bankrupt himself for any reduction in risk other than the complete elimination of the risk of death;

(2) for an increasing risk of death there is likely to be a range of probabilities for which no amount of compensation will induce the individual to increase his risk; and

(3) 'the marginal value of a decrease in risk from the initial risk level . . . is a non-decreasing function of initial risk' and that it is likely that it will be strictly increasing.

This last result is particularly important because it indicates the nature of the function with regard to small changes in risk levels around the existing levels. This is the situation which is likely to be relevant to most public sector decision-making in mortality changes. The other two are however consistent with *a priori* reasoning and are of value in that respect.

Jones-Lee then considers a single-period case for an insured individual and the continuous-time case whether or not the individual is insured. He concludes that the results for these three cases are all qualitatively the same as for the simple case and that 'a conventional cost-benefit analysis will tend to direct scarce safety improvement resources towards relatively high-income, low-life-expectancy areas'. Lest the former conclusion be misinterpreted Jones-Lee does indicate that 'a responsible social decision-maker would normally be expected to consider distributional effects together with the results of a cost-benefit analysis and not to base allocative decisions on the latter alone'.

In the light of the discussion of the question of 'objective' versus 'subjective' risk (see chapter 1, section 1.3.2) it is perhaps worth emphasising that Jones-Lee's analysis is concerned with subjective risk. He writes: 'Since individuals are hardly likely to view their own death or injury as the subject of repeated experiments, the preconditions for the existence of objective (relative frequency) probability measures would seem not to be fulfilled, and subjective probability therefore appears to be the relevant concept in the current context'.

Whether or not Jones-Lee's methodology is capable of yielding actual values will be discussed in section 7.5.5 below. What is clear from his analysis, however, is that the necessary theoretical background which is consistent with the cost-benefit framework outlined in the early chapters of this book has been successfully developed by Jones-Lee. This is a major contribution and should be recognised as such.

7.2.3 Mishan's Contribution

Mishan[13], while making no explicit reference to Jones-Lee, implicitly accepts much of what Jones-Lee states about the theoretical framework for valuation of life. He is critical of the many other types of methodology used in attempting to value life such as the gross output, the net output, the government revealed preference, and the life insurance approaches. (Many of these criticisms have been covered in chapters 5 and 6.)

Mishan's prime contribution is in placing the valuation of life very firmly in the theoretical framework of cost-benefit analysis. He writes[13]:

'If we are concerned, as we are in all allocative problems, with increasing society's satisfactions in some sense, and if in addition we eschew interpersonal comparisons of satisfactions, we can always be guided in the ranking of alternative economic arrangements by the notion of a Pareto improvement—an improvement such that at least one person is made better off and nobody is made worse off. A potential Pareto improvement, one in which the net gains *can* so be distributed that at least one person is made better off with none being made worse off, provides an alternative criterion, or definition, of social gain—one which, as it happens, provides the rationale of all familiar allocative propositions in economics, and therefore the rationale of all cost-benefit calculations'.

The logic of this leads us to consider how the problem of valuation of life can be phrased in such a way as to be consistent with the criteria laid down by Mishan, criteria which are fully accepted. It leads us to questions about compensation to individuals who are to 'sacrifice their lives in the interests of others'. There are situations in which it is known *ex ante* that there will be a number of persons killed as a result of some activity or other. For example, some immunisation programmes although yielding significant benefits sometimes cause the deaths of a few children through side-effects. While we will seldom if ever know *ex ante* who the victims will be, we will usually know within reasonable limits just how many lives will be 'expended' as part of the cost of pursuing such activities. But to pose the question to the potential victims, assuming they *were* identifiable, what compensation they would require to allow themselves to be sacrificed emphasises the need to move away from this 'absolute' valuation approach. For it is almost certainly the case that in most instances and for the great majority of people there will be no sum which the individual would accept in compensation for the loss of his life.

Fortunately this form of approach of compensation for death is not only impractical it is also wrong, at least in the vast majority of cases which are likely to be relevant to public sector decision-making. In most areas involving life at risk there is a very large element of uncertainty as far as any particular individual is concerned. While it may be predictable that about 15 000 males over 65 will die of lung cancer in England and Wales next year, there is for any single individual only a very small probability that he will be one of those who die. The question faced by the individual therefore is not one of certainty of death but the more easily handled one of a small risk of death. Once the problem is thus converted then it does become meaningful to talk in terms of compensation for accepting a risk of death of X where X is very much less than unity. There are of course problems as regards the extent to which individuals can conceive of small risks and small changes in such small risks—but this is something to which we will turn in more detail in section 7.3.

Mishan suggests that in the valuation of a reduction in risk approach we need to consider four types of risk. The first of these is the direct risk which people voluntarily assume. He maintains that the demand for any service, where a voluntary risk is assumed by the individuals who participate, already has built into it the cost of the risk. This in effect would mean that if the level of risk associated with the activity were reduced then the demand for the activity would be increased. This is undoubtedly true if we agree with Mishan's view that we must accept the individual's perception of the risk whether it be accurate or not but it need not hold if we relax this assumption. To the extent that individuals misperceive risk then there ought to be an adjustment made in the social welfare function to correct this misperception although possibly only with respect to that part of the welfare function which is concerned with reduction in risk *per se*. In that part which is concerned with the 'anxiety'-related welfare effect the individuals' perceptions may have to be taken as the base line because the level of anxiety will inevitably be a function of this perceived level of risk. (This issue of the separation of and different treatment of the two components of risk valuation is decribed in more detail in the next chapter.)

Mishan's second type of risk is of the direct involuntary form, the example of this which he quotes being the increased mortality arising from the disposal of radioactive waste material. In many instances it becomes very difficult to distinguish these first two types of risk as identified by Mishan. Much depends on one's starting point. It could be argued for example that all accidents at work are a result of 'voluntary' participation on the part of the victim in that there must have been some conscious choice on his part to work at that particular firm. But is the old lady knocked down while trying to cross a busy High Street putting herself at risk voluntary or involuntarily? Of course there are some activities where we can more easily argue that the risk was voluntarily chosen—mountaineering, potholing and smoking are some examples. But for very many cases the distinction between voluntary and involuntary may well turn out to be largely arbitrary. While we need not concern ourselves with this issue to the extent that Mishan does (because of his different view on the issue of perception), we still ignore it and we will return to the point again.

The other two types of risk which Mishan lists as being relevant are related to the question of concern for others. There are two aspects to this—the financial and the psychic. When an individual dies it can be argued that the rest of the community is financially affected although the change can be positive or negative. In most cases it is unlikely that this effect will have an impact on other than close friends and relatives of the deceased. The same is also true of the psychic element which simply reflects the fact that when someone we know (and like) dies then we suffer a certain loss of psychic welfare. (This type of consideration is akin to the 'subjective' costs of Dawson—see chapter 5, page 59.) The question of these 'others concerned' types of risk are central to the question of the individual private valuation of life as against the social valuation. This is an issue which raises some interesting points about the degree of interdependency between lives and how this should be catered for within any methodology of valuation. (Schelling[2] also distinguishes between the different groups of losers when an individual is killed—the individual himself, his family and friends and society as a whole. He makes the following interesting observation regarding the question of interdependencies between lives: 'If death takes a mother, a father, and two children, each from a different family, the consequences are different from the death of a family of four in a single accident. This is true both of the costs to society, because of the differential impact of dependents' care, and of the personal valuations within the family'. It is interesting to think of this for example in the context of the mass media which for some reason seems to give more prominence to the fact that whole families have been wiped out than that separate wives, husbands, sons and so on have been killed.) These issues are followed through in more detail in chapter 9.

7.2.4 *Conclusion*

Broadly then we find a good measure of agreement between the views of Jones-Lee, Mishan and Schelling and the criteria proposed in chapter 1 for valuation of life. They all emphasise the need to treat the question of valuation of life from an *ex ante* probabilistic standpoint and all are critical of the normal 'accounting' or 'human capital' type of approach. Further they are all in agreement that the valuation of a reduction in risk approach is the only one which is wholly defensible in theoretical economic terms.

7.3 SOME PROBLEMS IN PRACTICE

7.3.1 *The Small Probability Problem*

Turning to the question of *measurement* using the valuation of a reduction in risk approach, Jones-Lee, as indicated above, has suggested one way of tackling the problem and indeed has begun work on the practical side of coming up with actual numbers to place on the values (see section 7.5.5 below). What we do in this section is to point to some of the practical problems of using this type of methodology, before turning to some of the attempts which have been made to use the approach.

One problem which raises its head very quickly in this approach is that of how we deal with small probabilities. In most cases where public sector decision-makers are concerned with life saving or reduction in risk of death, the risk levels involved are very small and the reductions to be achieved by particular policy measures correspondingly even smaller. For example the risk of a male over the age of 65 dying from lung cancer in a year is only about 1 in 160. For the average pedestrian the risk of being killed on the roads in a year is only about 1 in 20 000. While these probabilities are small it has to be borne in mind that their respective contributions to the mortality rates are quite significant so that even smaller risks can be encountered. Such small probabilities as these have to be considered for a moment before they can be put in perspective and for some it may be virtually impossible to get them to comprehend what these probabilities mean. Schelling[2] for one concedes that there is a problem here but suggests the following type of methodology to deal with it—his 'scaling of risk' approach: 'A man who cannot get to grips with one chance in 1000 of death may be able to come to grips with one chance in 10, or vice versa. He is asked, for example, what reduction in income after taxes he would incur in perpetuity to avoid a 10 per cent chance of death ...'.

Schelling suggests that he may be able to say that he will sacrifice a third of his income to avoid this risk. He is doubtful if we can simply move from this to a risk of 1 in 1000 by dividing by 100 to give an

97

amount of 1/300 of his income because, he argues, 'a loss of 0.33 per cent of his income will not look one-hundredth as bad to him as the loss of 33 per cent of his income'. Schelling continues: 'He might ... be asked what fraction of his income he would give up to avoid a one-tenth chance of losing one-third of his income'. He maintains that this is an 'ordinary insurance decision' which the individual will be able to answer.

Schelling's approach of 'scaling of risk' neatly takes care of the problem of diminishing marginal utility of income, that is the view that the utility obtained from each additional £1 of income falls. At the same time it would appear to leave untouched the possible non-linearity of the value of reduction in risk function, in other words that the value attached to a reduction in risk of x will not necessarily be constant but be dependent on the existing level of risk. Of course, if over the relevant range the function approximates to linearity then there is little problem. We simply do not know how great the departure from linearity is—if it exists at all—although we may suspect that it is sufficiently great for us to be wary of ignoring it completely. The essential point at issue here is that abstracting from the question of actually paying for the reduction in risk—and thus abstracting from the marginal utility of income issue—would the level of 'abhorrence' which a man feels at the prospect of a risk of death of 1 in 10 be exactly ten times that which he would feel in the case of a risk of 1 in 100? While it is difficult to offer proof on this point without some empirical research there are sufficient grounds for questioning the linearity theorem and hence cast doubt on whether Schelling's 'scaling of risks' procedure adequately solves the problem of small probabilities.

7.3.2 *Private Behavioural versus Hypothetical Questioning*

But do we really require to look to some interview technique involving the posing of largely hypothetical questions to individuals to put the valuation of a reduction in risk approach into practice? Can we not study individual behaviour and determine from that what value is placed by different individuals on different levels of risk reduction? As Drèze[1] proposes (although he does not want to be interpreted literally)—ought not the engineers of the *'ponts et chaussées'* and all other decision-makers concerned with life-saving activities to observe such matters as the use or non-use of safety belts and other such life-saving behaviour by individuals?

Individuals do frequently take actions to reduce their risk of death. Such actions may involve a purchase of some good which has a direct effect on risk (a seat belt, for example) or it may involve some trade-off with time or some other not directly money-valued factor. For example, if we were to follow through in detail the arguments which a commuter might use in deciding which mode of transport to use in travelling to work, we might find that he would consider each of the modes available in turn in terms of total trip time, comfort and reliability, the financial cost and the risk of death or injury on the trip. Normally it will be unlikely that a unique optimum choice exists in terms of there being one mode which consistently comes out on top on all counts. Except when this happens there will be a need to trade-off such elements as x minutes saved in travel time against less comfort and £y more per year in fares. The type of trade-off that we would be interested in would be the trade-off between risk of death and one of the other elements in the decision, for example reduced risk of death (or injury) 'bought' through increased fares (or direct financial trade-off) longer journey time or increased inconvenience (or indirect trade-offs which need to be further analysed before the trade-off can be made in money terms).

One of the principal advantages of this type of approach is that it yields direct 'on the spot' values of changes in risk. Thus not only are the values which emerge related directly to individual consumers' preferences (which we have previously argued is desirable in any valuation methodology which is to be based in cost-benefit analysis) but also the values can take direct account of any positive utility in risk taking. Normally we would assume that all persons are risk 'averters' although as between individuals there may be variations in their degrees of risk aversion. This is most likely to be the case in the example of routine travelling used above and in most respects it is true of the field of health.

It is worth mentioning the example of smoking at this juncture. We can assume that the great majority of smokers smoke because they enjoy it, or they obtain some benefit from their cigarettes. While the example is bedevilled by the addictive nature of nicotine nonetheless we can assume that in so far as the smoker is aware of the costs involved he obtains a positive net benefit from his smoking (in other words the benefits outweigh the costs) otherwise he would not smoke. However, in so far as we are interested here in the question of utility of risk-taking it is only if the smoker actually gets some sense of

99

satisfaction from taking a risk in smoking that there is 'risk loving' on the part of our smoker. Thus we need to draw a distinction between doing something which involves risk but which also gives pleasure, from doing something involving risk as a result of which part of the satisfaction is in the risk associated with it.

Situations do arise where there would appear to be elements of enjoyment in risk-taking—motorcycling, mountaineering, potholing, among other activities. It is important that we do not neglect this element, but normally we can assume for our purposes that no element of enjoyment in risk-taking is present. (It is difficult to imagine that an octogenarian attempting to cross the Strand will get much joy from dodging between cars bearing down on him on all sides!) But there will be these other cases where the element of positive utility in risk-taking is of relevance although it is difficult to forecast how important it will be. Bernoulli maintained[14]: 'It becomes evident that no valid measurement of the value of a risk can be obtained without consideration being given to its utility'. The 'private behavioural' approach would in effect 'build in' this element. (With all other factors equal other than risk and money cost an individual might be prepared to travel by a higher risk mode even when that mode is also the more expensive financially.)

However, there are difficulties in using the 'private behavioural' approach to valuation of mortality risk reduction. The first require-ment that has to be met for the method to be fully operational is that the individuals whose behaviour is to be studied are perfectly knowledgeable about the levels of risk involved in their reaching a decision. In the case of private decisions, of course, an individual will normally reach a decision about any 'purchase' on the basis of his existing knowledge or else he will invest some time or resources in improving his state of knowledge. The man who buys a house has to decide whether he thinks it is worth paying to have a professional surveyor inspect the house for structural damage, rot or other defects. The older the property the greater the risk that there is something structurally wrong with it, and therefore the more likely is the potential purchaser to employ a surveyor. But no one other than the potential purchaser is involved in the decision whether or not to have the property surveyed. It is by and large immaterial to the decision whether the purchaser has made a correct estimate of the likelihood of there being structural damage and of the surveyor finding it. Why then in the case of life saving do we adopt a different standpoint?

Obviously how a commuter decides to go to work will be only marginally affected by the differentials in the levels of risk associated with the different modes of travel open to him. Also in most cases this decision will be taken by the commuter on the basis of his existing knowledge of the factors such as the level of risk of death by different modes. These 'private' choices ought rightly to be left to the individuals concerned—although even here there may be a case for an education programme on the comparative risk levels involved in the different modes.

Where the situation moves away from being a private decision —with the involvement of public financing, questions of externalities arising (that is effects on others) the problem of equity considerations becoming of relevance, etc.—then there emerges a strong case for arguing that in the interests of a better allocation of resources (particularly *ex post*) imperfections of knowledge on the part of individuals ought not to be tolerated. They ought to be replaced by more objective and more accurate estimates where these are available.

The outstanding reason for arguing for a replacement of misperceived estimates of risk levels by improved ones is basically that individuals are sufficiently aware of their shortcomings on knowledge in some circumstances to be prepared to accept that *ex post* they are likely to be better off if they accept the judgment of 'the experts'. It is the awareness of this gap between the individual's perceived benefit *ex ante* and *ex post* by the individual himself that allows the proposal to be made that the individual is prepared to have his own estimation overruled, in other words the individual is prepared to accept an element of state paternalism. In effect this amounts to arguing that the individual acting in his own best interests accepts that it is better to let 'the experts' make some decisions on his behalf. Thus it is not that the good of life saving is different in itself it is that life saving is an area where this abrogation by the individual to 'the experts' is the way in which the individual decides what is in his own best interests. (This question of perception is of considerable importance and is discussed much more fully in chapter 9.)

A further and more practical difficulty arises from the paucity of situations which lend themselves to study by this 'private behavioural' approach. There are comparatively few situations where the necessary factors can be identified and individuals' behaviour studied in the required detail to allow the valuation process to proceed. None the less some case studies are reported upon in section 7.5 below.

101

Nevertheless where such few examples as exist could prove to be of value would be as a check on the valuations emerging from the type of approach embodied in the Jones-Lee methodology. For example, if the Jones-Lee approach were applied to construction workers receiving danger money for height work then it might prove possible to use the risk (or more likely perceived risk) and the danger money paid as a basis for checking the results obtained from applying the Jones-Lee approach. Should a reasonable degree of agreement emerge from this and any other similar examples of such comparisons, then it might be possible to generalise beyond those areas where 'behavioural' type checks could be applied and claim that the Jones-Lee valuations held generally.

In any empirical study devised to obtain values from the reduction in risk form of approach it is therefore most likely that it will need to be tackled primarily through some form of interview technique involving the asking of individuals some rather hypothetical questions, as Jones-Lee suggests within his approach. There are, however, several difficulties in this area. Firstly in many respects in dealing with reductions in risk of death we are dealing with a good which if not wholly a public good (see page 17) at least has many of the attributes—and hence from a valuation point of view many of the disadvantages—of being a public good. With public goods there is a difficulty in getting individuals to reveal their true preferences. (This follows because of the fact that even if they value the good highly there is little private advantage to them in revealing their true strength of preference for the good.)

Secondly, even if the public goods difficulty can be overcome, it may not be possible to devise a method of interviewing which can be made meaningful to the interviewees. Aside from the difficulties (already touched on) associated with the comprehension of small probabilities, this is an area of research where individuals interviewed may have some form of mental block. They may simply be unable or in some cases unwilling to even try to think rationally about the taboo area of death.

Thirdly there is the fundamental problem of using the answers to hypothetical questions as a proxy for what perfectly informed people would think or do in practice. (By inserting 'perfectly informed' at this point we overcome the problem associated with individuals' thinking on actions to be taken being based on misperceptions of risk. The point therefore remains that even if fully informed there might still be some difference between what emerges from the hypothetical and the reality.) Generally in economics we attempt to obtain information about individuals' preferences through studying their behaviour in the market place. Where this normal form of study appears to be deficient and have considerable difficulties associated with it, and we have to resort to hypothetical questions to elicit the information we require, there must be some doubt about the extent to which we are obtaining answers which genuinely reflect the individuals' preferences. Nor is it apparent how we could easily introduce some form of checking mechanism which would allow us to see whether our results were reasonably accurate and valid—other than the check discussed immediately above.

7.4 CONCLUSION

Despite these very real difficulties there is so much to be said for this type of methodology both in terms of economic theory and in being readily seen to be a rational and sensible approach that we ought not to be too obsessed with the practical difficulties of actually establishing values. Jones-Lee has suggested one way of arriving at actual values. With this exception, however, little consideration has been given to the question of obtaining the actual values. This is hardly surprising given the relative youthfulness of the underlying theoretical structure—the valuation of reduction of risk of death. What does seem right is to at least start with what is a theoretically sound method and to move to the problems of actually obtaining values rather than to continue as in the past with a methodology for which the main virtue has been the ease of application in obtaining values and the main vice the lack of an acceptable economic rationale.

7.5 SOME CASE STUDIES

7.5.1 *Danger Money*

In some industries (such as the construction industry) extra remuneration is paid to individuals who undertake work which is considered to be hazardous. Certain national agreements are laid down regarding the size of this extra remuneration but by and large these national agreements are lower limits and it is normally the case that higher remuneration is paid at individual sites. These latter rates

103

are usually negotiated at site level. It is obviously of some interest what these rates are because if we could establish some trade-off between increased risk and these extra payments, we might be in a position to establish the value of risk in these circumstances. This type of approach may be seen largely as belonging to the 'private behavioural' category although in this particular case the 'behaviour' with which we are concerned is not so much individually orientated as group determined.

As with all approaches belonging to this category we have of course the problem of measuring the increased risk accepted by the individuals at risk. Our interest lies not in the actual or objective assessment of risk but in the level of risk as perceived by the men involved. The question to which we seek an answer therefore is: how much money is required by individuals to accept a higher perceived risk?

Some information has been published through the N.E.D.C.[15] on extra remuneration in hazardous occupations. Height money is paid under nationally negotiated agreements on certain bases. Table 7.1, for example, provides an indication of height money paid in a few situations.

Table 7.1 *Height money paid in certain agreed circumstances*

Steam generating plant erection agreement		*Site agreement at Coryton*		*Site agreement at Grangemouth*	
Height (ft)	Scale of allowance per hour (p)	Height (ft)	Scale of allowance per hour (p)	Height (ft)	Scale of allowance per hour (p)
50–75	$\frac{5}{6}$	30–75	$\frac{5}{6}$	30–60	$\frac{5}{6}$
75–100	$1\frac{2}{3}$	75–100	$1\frac{2}{3}$	60–90	$1\frac{2}{3}$
100–150	$2\frac{1}{2}$	100–150	$2\frac{1}{2}$	90–120	$2\frac{1}{2}$
150–200	5	150–200	5	120–150	$3\frac{1}{3}$
(an additional $2\frac{1}{2}$p each additional 50 ft)		(an additional $2\frac{1}{2}$p each additional 50 ft)		(an additional $\frac{2}{3}$p for each additional 30 ft)	

Now if it were possible to determine the accident risk level in these situations at ground level and at various heights, and if we could assume that actual risk levels and perceived risk levels were the same then we could establish the trade-off between increases in perceived risk and compensation for accepting these risks through the payment of the above sums. This has not proved possible in that all the information obtained relates to the fatal accident risk rate in the construction industry as a whole (67 deaths per 10^8 hours exposure—compared to four per 10^8 hours exposure for British industry as a whole—according to Kletz[16]). Even if it proved possible to get more detailed information regarding the level of risk involved it is doubtful if we could hope to get very accurate information about the levels of exposure at different heights. It would also be difficult without a special survey to get any indication whether the assumption of equating the objectively assessed level of risk with that perceived by the men at risk is accurate.

Purely as an example however we can make the following assumptions

(1) the accident death-rate at ground level in the construction industry is 50 per 10^8 hours exposure;

(2) the accident death-rate at 50–75 ft is 100;

(3) the non-fatal accident rate is the same at all heights;

(4) the extra remuneration required to work at heights is as in the steam generating plant erection agreement (see table 7.1);

(5) perceived risk equals actual risk;

Then the risk of death on the ground per man week is

$$50 \times 40 \times 10^{-8} = 2 \times 10^{-5};$$

and the risk of death at 50–75 ft per man week is

$$100 \times 40 \times 10^{-8} = 4 \times 10^{-5}$$

Over a 40-hour week the amount of pre-tax 'height money' paid will be 40 × 0.87p, or 33p. At a rate of tax of 30 per cent, post tax this is equivalent to 23p.

Thus for every additional man killed at 50–75 ft (that is, additional to the number who would have been killed had they been working at ground level) the amount of extra remuneration paid after tax is £0.23 × $(1/2 \times 10^{-5})$ = £11 500 which might be taken on the basis of the assumptions made as the value of life—the equivalence of one statistical life in the construction industry for men working at a height of 50–75 ft. (It is likely that at other heights the relationship between risk and remuneration will not remain constant and consequently the 'value of life' will be different at different heights.)

105

The principal disadvantages of this method are simply that it requires rather detailed data of a kind not normally available—the level of subjectively assessed risk at different heights, the actual remuneration (as opposed to the nationally agreed minima) for accepting work in hazardous situations, and the relationship between non-fatal and fatal risk and the individual workers' relative assessments of these risks. Even if all these data were available we would still be faced with the difficulty that for the method to operate in an ideal way we would require a perfectly competitive labour market. Further, in generalising from this type of analysis we would need to show that people working in hazardous occupations had the same attitudes to risk as the general populace—a most unlikely outcome, because if construction workers tended to ignore or underperceive risk and the rest of the community did not, then the valuation of construction workers could not be used for the population as a whole.

7.5.2 *Life Insurance*

Life insurance cover is another way of attempting to use the 'private behavioural' approach to value life. In so far as an individual foregoes present consumption (to pay premiums) to insure his life then the sum payable on his death might be assumed to be some measure of the value of his life. By definition, however, the sum insured is only payable on the death of the insured person. The most that can be said of the amount of cover is that it might be considered to be some estimate by the insured of the value of his life to his dependents (which is of course of some relevance to life valuation) but it tells us nothing about the value of life to the insured himself.

The essential ingredient missing from this type of approach is that while we are interested in evaluation from the point of view of reducing risk of death, life insurance has no direct effect on mortality risk. (It is conceivable that it could raise the risk of death indirectly if by covering himself for life insurance an individual has a reduced aversion to risk. An extreme example of this is where some insurance companies do not pay out on life cover in the event of death from suicide within two years of cover commencing).

Perhaps just as fundamental is that in terms of providing some sort of reasonable standard of living for dependents in the event of the insured's death, it is patently obvious that the average level of life insurance cover—even if we restrict our population to insured lives—is well below what it 'ought' to be (if we define this level as providing a sufficient income on which his dependents are to survive). Further, to base any analysis on the insured population alone is almost certainly to choose a biased sample. When we step back from this approach and consider the rationale of insurance it becomes apparent that all we are really attempting to obtain by this approach is some measure of the financial dependency of certain individuals (normally a wife and children) on a 'bread-winner'. Putting it in these terms merely serves to emphasise that if we do seek such a measure of financial dependency then there are obviously much more straightforward ways of obtaining it than resorting to what in the event appears the rather obscure approach of life insurance cover.

7.5.3 *Melinek's Cases*

Melinek[17] has examined a number of areas where individuals' behaviour in risk situations may reveal life valuations. Two of these relate to road safety—driving speed and the use of pedestrian subways.

Since speed limits reduce fatal accidents by about 15 per cent and average speed by about 5 per cent Melinek suggests that on average a motorist is prepared to increase his risk of a fatal accident by 15 per cent in order to save 5 per cent of his journey time. Hence for a 1 per cent saving on time he suggests the motorist will be willing to accept a 3 per cent increase in risk of a fatal accident.

Now if we equate the savings in time with the cost of additional fatalities this provides a method of determining the upper limit of value of life. Thus the saving in time is

$$0.01 \, sv/S$$

where s = distance travelled; v = value put on unit time saved; S = average speed.

The increase in the number of road deaths is

$$0.03 \eta_d$$

where η_d = number of road accident deaths.

Then the implied value of life is given by

$$\frac{sv}{3S\eta_d}$$

Inserting appropriate values Melinek estimates the value of life to be £73 500.

In his example of pedestrian subways Melinek quotes evidence which shows that most pedestrians will only use a subway if it takes less than 27 per cent more time than crossing the road. He then takes the value of life as being equal to

$$\frac{Vt_c}{P_aP_d}$$

where v = value of unit of time saved; t_c = extra time pedestrians are willing to spend to avoid risk from crossing the road; P_a = probability of an accident when crossing the road; P_d = probability of these accidents being fatal.

Inserting the appropriate figures, the value of life emerges as £86 500.

7.5.4 *Motorway Driving Behaviour*

In an interesting approach to the question of behaviour in a life-threatening situation Ghosh et al.[18] examine the relationships between speed, accidents and petrol consumption on motorways. An individual driver can, within certain limits, choose his motorway speed. The faster he goes the more time he will save but the more petrol he will consume. He may also increase his likelihood of an accident.

Now if we assume that the valuation of life and limbs is known (using Dawson's values, for example) and we know the price of petrol, if we also assume that the average speed on motorways is the optimal speed then we can obtain the value of time. Indeed if we know or can assume any three of the optimal speed, the price of petrol, the value of time and the value of accidents then we can obtain the fourth.

When the optimal speed is assumed equal to the actual average of 58.8 m.p.h., petrol is assumed to cost 35p per gallon and £1.00 per hour is taken as the value of time, Ghosh et al. obtain a value of life of £94 000. To arrive at life as opposed to an average casualty they use weights derived from the Transport and Road Research Laboratory values for slight, serious and fatal casualties. They also determine that on the same basis if the value of time falls to 63p an hour the implied value of life is zero and any further fall in the time value results of course in a negative value of life.

7.5.5 Jones-Lee's Questionnaire

Jones-Lee has outlined and tested an experimental procedure which provides one possible method of obtaining quantified estimates of the values of reductions in risk of death. The procedure consists of inviting individuals to complete a questionnaire on the value of safety in which they can 'trade-off' safety and wealth, that is, it provides quantified estimates for the theoretical model outlined in section 7.2.2 above.

The individual was confronted with a choice between two airlines which differed only in respect of their recent safety record and their fares. Given a fixed fare and a known safety record for the one airline, the individual was asked at what fare he would just be induced to fly by the other airline, assuming some different safety records for the other airline. This Jones-Lee uses to obtain 'short-period' estimates of the value of a small change in risk of death. Thus for an individual who indicated that he would just be induced to travel by one airline if the fare was £105 and the safety record was one fatal crash in 500 000 flights, rather than the other airline at £100 where the safety record was twice as bad, then the value of the reduction risk of 1 in 500 000 is £5 and the 'value of life' in this particular instance £2.5 million (or £5 × 500 000).

In addition, to obtain 'long-run' estimates the subjects were asked about a job-location decision in which the individual is indifferent between the two locations except for house prices and the effect of environmental pollution on life expectancy. In a similar manner to the airline Jones-Lee then asked the respondents to trade-off house prices and life expectancy.

Jones-Lee does highlight some of the possible objections to his procedure—the fact that the individual in the 'direct inquiry' approach has to imagine situations rather than actually experience them and the difficulties of subjective probabilities. In addition, and not unexpectedly, following the discussion above, some of the respondents appear to have had some difficulty in handling small probabilities.

(The fact that Jones-Lee only had a response rate of 33 per cent from a sample of academics, research workers and public sector employees is particularly worrying—especially if it was due to difficulties of understanding or perception.)

While the procedure is one which, if capable of being applied successfully, would allow the major theme of this book to be translated into the estimation of actual values, there are sufficient doubts regarding some of the empirical aspects of Jones-Lee's work to make it questionable whether the methodology can yield actual, acceptable, reliable values. This is particularly true of the issues of subjective probabilities and the 'anxiety' aspect of risk reduction (which is considered at length in the next chapter). But given the very recent emergence from darkness to light of thinking on life valuation, these early attempts of Jones-Lee to develop this experimental procedure are encouraging.

7.5.6 *Needleman's Valuation of Other People's Lives*

Needleman's[19] starting point is that as regards public authorities investing in life-saving policies 'there appears to be agreement among recent writers . . . that the maximum amount it is worth spending . . . is the total valuation put on the reductions in the probability of dying by the individuals at risk, their relatives and friends and other people concerned for their safety'. The question he addresses is not that of valuing reductions in risk for those at risk but how much the relatives of those at risk are prepared to pay for reductions in risk for those at risk.

Needleman's basic premise is that 'if individuals are prepared to increase their own risk of dying in order to reduce another's risk . . . and if they are also prepared to pay to reduce their own risk, then that implies . . . that they are prepared to pay to reduce another's risk'.

In a similar model to that of Jones-Lee, Needleman assumes that the amount that an individual k would be prepared to pay to reduce the risk of death for another individual j would be a function of k's wealth and of k's concern for j's safety. This he calls 'the coefficient of concern'. This 'represents the lowest rate of trade-off that is acceptable to k between changes in his risk and changes in j's risk when both he and j are facing the same initial level of risk'.

Needleman's expression for the ratio of the average valuation of each set of relatives to the average valuation of those at risk is

$$\frac{1}{\bar{W}_j} \cdot N_j \cdot H_k \cdot C$$

where $\bar{W}_j$ is the average wealth of those at risk; N_j is a matrix of elements representing the number of individuals of a particular sex in the ath age group at risk as a proportion of the total number of individuals at risk; H_k is a matrix of elements representing numbers of relatives of those at risk together with the average wealth of these relatives; and C is a matrix of elements representing average coefficients of concern for the relatives at risk for different relationship groups.

As a source of some empirical evidence from which to try to determine the values of coefficients of concern Needleman looks at kidney transplants. Potential donors, who decide for themselves whether to proceed or not, are informed about the changes in risks for both donors and recipients of kidneys. In this context Needleman attempts to measure and quantify the various elements listed above. He derives table 7.2, using various assumptions to plug certain gaps in the data.

Table 7.2   *The valuations of relationship groups*

Relationship group	Valuation of relationship group as a percentage of the total valuation of all relatives (%)
Grandparents	7.8
Parents	38.6
Aunts and uncles	5.8
Spouse	16.8
Siblings	13.4
First cousins	5.2
Children	9.6
Nieces and nephews	2.2
Grandchildren	0.4
Total	100.0

This particular approach of Needleman's, based as it is in the reduction in risk valuation school, is important not only in its acceptance of the framework of risk reduction but in applying it to *other* people's lives. It would be wrong to try to generalise too far on the basis of Needleman's single example of kidney transplants but it is the approach *per se* that must be welcomed.

7.5.7 Conclusion on Case Studies

This type of approach would seem worthy of wider research. If more of these case studies can be examined then a more general picture of life values from private behavioural patterns may emerge. In addition, however, some research directed at perception would appear desirable. As it stands the model of Ghosh *et al.* only estimates life values as accurately as individuals perceive the relationships between speed, accidents, time and running costs. Research into such perceptions would help to clarify the potential value of the type of model adopted by Ghosh and his colleagues. Similarly, knowledge of the accuracy of perception of risk by construction workers, and in Melinek's study by drivers and pedestrians, is crucial to the validity of any answers which might emerge from such studies.

But it is in the Jones-Lee approach and that of Needleman that the most fruitful line of investigation appears to lie. There remain various problems, but the fact that such empirical applications of the value of reduction in risk approach are following as rapidly in the wake of recent theoretical developments is encouraging.

REFERENCES

1. Drèze, J., L'utilité sociale d'une vie humaine, *Rev. Franc. Rech. Oper.* (1962)
2. Schelling, T. C., The life you save may be your own. In *Problems in Public Expenditure Analysis*, ed. S. B. Chase, Brookings Institute, Washington (1968)
3. Zeckhauser, R., Uncertainty and the need for collective action. In *Public Expenditure and Policy Analysis*, ed. R. H. Haveman and J. Margolis, Markham Publishing Company, Chicago (1970)
4. Bailey, M., Comment on Schelling. In *Problems in Public Expenditure Analysis*, ed. S. B. Chase, Brookings Institute, Washington (1968)
5. Jones-Lee, M. W., Valuation of reduction in probability of death by road accident, *J. Transport Econ. Pol.*, Jan. (1969)
6. Jones-Lee, M. W., The value of changes in the probability of death or injury, *J. Polit. Econ.*, **82**, No. 4, 835–850, Aug. (1974)
7. Jones-Lee, M. W., *The Value of Life. An Economic Analysis*, Martin Robertson, London (1976)
8. Hirshleifer, J., Investment decisions under uncertainty–choice–theoretic approaches, *Q. J. Econ.*, May (1966)

9. Ramsey, F. P., *The Foundations of Mathematics and Other Logical Essays*, Kegan Paul, London (1931)

10. Savage, L. J., *The Foundations of Statistics*, Wiley, New York (1954)

11. Shackle, G. L. S., *Expectation in Economics*, Cambridge University Press, Cambridge (1949)

12. von Neumann, J., and Morgenstern, O., *Theory of Games and Economic Behaviour*, Princeton University Press, New Jersey (1953)

13. Mishan, E. J., *Cost Benefit Analysis*, George Allen and Unwin, London, chapters 22 and 23 (1971)

14. Bernoulli, D., Exposition of a new theory on the measurement of risk. Reproduced in *Econometrica*, Jan. (1954)

15. *Large Industrial Sites*, National Economic Development Council, HMSO (1970)

16. Kletz, T. A., *Hazard Analysis: A Quantitative Approach to Safety*, ICI (1968)

17. Melinek, S. J., A method of evaluating human life for economic purposes, *Accident Anal. Prev.*, Oct. (1974)

18. Ghosh, D., Lees, D., and Seal, W., Optimal motorway speed and some valuations of time and life, *Manchester School Econ. Soc. Stud.*, **43**, No. 2, 134–143, June (1975)

19. Needleman, L., Valuing other people's lives. In *Manchester School Econ. Soc. Stud.*, 309–342, Dec. (1976)

8

The Preferred Valuation Methodology Again: Option Values and 'PIP' Goods

8.1 TWO ASPECTS OF RISK

8.1.1 *Introduction*

As chapter 7 has already indicated there appear to be two elements involved in reducing risk and in the values to be placed on such reductions. Let us call these two elements R_i and R_{ii}. R_i is concerned solely with risk reduction *per se*. It is that element associated with a reduction in risk of death which is not related to fear or anxiety but solely to the loss associated with death.

In addition to this element most of us of course have some fear of death. Separate from the desire to live longer is the fear of death itself—partly the anxiety associated with the act of death and partly the anxiety of wondering what the state of death is really like, (for example, is it 'the end'? Is there an afterlife?). This 'anxiety related' element is labelled R_{ii}.

8.1.2 *Risk Reduction per se*

In so far as separation of these two elements is valid—and it is only as an analytical aid that we are interested in the separation—then several useful points can be made. Firstly as far as R_i is concerned it is likely that the loss associated with some level of risk of death will be in direct proportion to the level of risk. This is equivalent to assuming that V_i, the loss associated with death itself, is independent of the level of risk. Thus in terms of R_i alone an individual would be indifferent between having his risk of death reduced from 0.8 to 0.7 or from 0.3 to 0.2; or

114

again a reduction in risk from 0.2 to 0.1 would be ten times as valuable as a reduction from 0.4 to 0.39—all in terms of R_i alone. In so far as the concept of R_i is valid then it suggests that for a specific individual, once the valuation of reduction in risk *per se* is known for one change in risk, then it is a simple matter of proportionality to obtain any other. This arises because of the postulated linear relationship in the valuation of risk. Schelling[1] concedes that there may well be just such a relationship when he writes: 'there are good reasons for considering the worth of risk-reduction to be proportionate to the absolute reduction of risk, for considering a reduction of 10 per cent to 9 per cent about equivalent to a reduction from 5 per cent to 4 per cent'. (Schelling is writing here solely in terms of the equivalent of our R_i.) While accepting this view of Schelling's we must accept that when comparing very different sizes of changes in risk and consequently very different sizes of values for these changes then we may well have to adjust our postulated linear relationship to allow for the diminishing marginal utility of income—as was discussed in chapter 7.

8.1.3 *Anxiety Associated with Risk*

Turning now to the element R_{ii}, this factor is not related to risk *per se* but to the anxiety associated with risk and conversely the increased peace of mind associated with reduced risk. It might be termed the 'fear' factor. The assumption made is that with regard to risk of death, apart from the actual expected loss associated with losing life, there is in addition a theoretically separate force at work which is related to the anticipation of dying, the fear of death, etc. This feature is a more subjective one and as such is less likely to exhibit the linear relationships associated with R_i. It is this factor which will explain the fact that for valuations of reductions in risk *in toto* the relationship may not be linear—for example, reductions of 0.1 from 0.8 and from 0.3 not being given equal values. It is also hypothesised that it explains why different values may emerge for equal reductions in risk from equal existing risk levels where the only factor which varies is the mode of death, for example road accident death as opposed to cancer death. In this type of situation then if the individual at risk has a greater fear of death from cancer than death in a road accident then this will become apparent in the R_{ii} value. In effect by introducing this latter element we can use it to explain possibly all the apparent irrationalities which exist in this area of differential valuations of risk reduction.

This 'fear' factor, R_{ii}, of course only makes sense in an *ex ante* context. For the individual victim, death *ex post* can be considered as being completely homogeneous. (Proof here would be difficult—but it seems a not unreasonable assumption to make!) *Ex ante* what we are in effect suggesting is that theoretically we can separate these two factors R_i and R_{ii} and propose a method of valuation of risk of death which assumes a linear relationship for R_i but not necessarily for R_{ii}.

8.2   POSSIBLE THEORETICAL APPROACHES

8.2.1 *Option Values and Option Demand*

There are some interesting parallels between, on the one hand, these ideas of R_i, risk *per se* and R_{ii}, the anxiety associated with risk, and on the other some of the concepts associated with 'option values' and 'option demand'. Weisbrod[2] first coined the term 'option value' to describe willingness to pay for the option to consume some commodity or service in the future. He pointed to the fact that 'a number of significant commodities exist which are apparently of a pure individual-consumption variety, but which also possess characteristics of a pure collective-consumption good'.

As an example of this type of good, Weisbrod takes the case of a privately owned park, entry to which is by admission fees. If total costs are greater than revenue then the park should be closed (both on private and social efficiency grounds if certain assumptions are made). However there may well be individuals who believe they may use the park at some time in the future and who will be prepared to pay some sum to try to keep the option and hence the park open. Weisbrod argues that in deciding whether or not to keep the park open the existence of this 'option value' ought to be taken into account. (Of course in attempting in the private market to collect the revenue from this option value we would be up against the 'public goods' problem of persuading individuals to reveal their true preferences.) Weisbrod suggests that the park 'may be thought of as producing two outputs: services of an individual-consumption sort to actual users, and stand-by, or option, services of a collective-consumption sort to non-users'. It is of course possible to consider a situation in which there is no demand for the first type of output (in other words, no one currently makes use of the facility) but the second type of demand still existing and conceivably to an extent sufficient to justify keeping the park open. (A further example quoted by Weisbrod—and more in our line of inquiry—is that of hospitals which at any point in time perform a function directly for the few and a function of a stand-by kind for the many.)

Weisbrod also states that 'infrequency and uncertainty of purchase are not the only conditions bringing about a potential deviation of optimal private from optimal social behaviour' in this type of situation. Another requirement is that 'expansion or recommencement of production at the time any occasional purchasers wish to make a purchase must be difficult (in time or resources) or impossible'.

The concept of option demand can in theory be applied to many goods. What makes it more relevant and of more significance in some cases rather than others is the level of frequency of purchase and the degree of reproducibility of the good. In some cases option demand will be less relevant to a decision in that actual current demand (or user demand) will be sufficient on its own to justify the continued supply of the good in question and in such cases option demand can be met at no additional cost.

Demand of the kind in which we are particularly interested in the field of life saving is in many ways similar to that for the types of goods discussed by Weisbrod. For example, the low probabilies that a particular individual will be involved in an accident on any particular day and the randomness in selection of accident victims are features which are very much in common with Weisbrod's 'infrequency and uncertainty' conditions which he states as applicable to these option demand goods. The impossibility of, or difficulty in, recommencement of production has its parallel in the life-saving case where the reproducibility which is in question is that of the life of the individual concerned. One difference however does exist in the parallels being drawn here. In Weisbrod's example of the option value of visiting a park the individual concerned will know whether he has visited the park or not; in the case of life saving the individual will frequently be completely unaware that the option has been exercised. Fortunately this does not alter the relevance of the option demand concept because just as it is immaterial whether the park visiting option is ever exercised so it is immaterial whether the 'protection' option is exercised or not. Consequently it is immaterial whether the individual is aware of whether the option has been exercised or not.

8.2.2 *PIP Goods*

Before pursuing the question of option demand and its relevance further, let us consider a later article by Zeckhauser[3]. In a section entitled 'Collective Provision with Individual's Preferences Uncertain' Zeckhauser suggests that 'an individual will rarely be able to determine exactly his future level of demand for a good ... He would have to know whether he would be involved in an accident before he could estimate his need for hospital accident emergency room'. Zeckhauser is concerned with what he calls 'PIP' goods (probabilistic individual preferences) which he defines as 'goods which by their very nature make accurate prediction of future preferences impossible'.

Zeckhauser emphasises that PIP goods are frequently concerned with prevention of one sort or another—crime prevention, immunisation against diseases, etc. The similarity to Weisbrod's concept of option values is obvious, although Zeckhauser argues against Weisbrod on the question of the magnitude of option values. He suggests: 'if an economic man will be faced with perfect price discrimination, should he be interested in consuming the good, he will be indifferent whether or not he purchases it. He will not be able to reap any consumer's surplus at the time of purchase; the availability of the good will in no way be able to increase his welfare. His option value to keep the purchase available will be zero'.

However, Zeckhauser has failed to grasp the significance for option values of the concept of 'value in anticipation'. The fact that at time $t_0 + n$ an individual will pay £x as a maximum for the purchase of a good does not mean that it thereby follows that if he *has* to pay £x at time $t_0 + n$ he will not be prepared to pay some sum *in addition* at time t_0 to keep the option open to purchase at time $t_0 + n$. Defined in this way the value in anticipation is something which can only be obtained in advance of the purchase of the good. It is therefore derived from utility which is obtained in the period between t_0 and $t_0 + n$. Any utility obtained thereafter is derived from utility in use and is the form of utility more commonly found in standard economic theory. At the point of purchase—and hence considering only utility in use—Zeckhauser's position is valid. It is only when we re-examine the situation at time t_0 rather than $t_0 + n$ that the value in anticipation comes into play and adds a new dimension to value and one which, as Weisbrod suggests, is relevant to the application of consumer theory in these types of situations. It is only by ignoring the value in anticipation concept that Zeckhauser's position can be made tenable.

The idea of bringing risk-spreading into the picture takes Zeckhauser's analysis further than Weisbrod's. To illustrate the risk-spreading concept within the framework of the PIP goods Zeckhauser takes the example of a community of 100 individuals, identical in every way including the fact that they all own houses which they value at $10 000. One house is burnt down each year. The annual rental for a fire engine which prevents any damage to a burning house is $12 000. In such circumstances the community would decide not to rent the fire engine. It would be cheaper for all of them to pay towards the reconstruction of the annually destroyed house.

Zeckhauser continues

> the individuals within the community are risk averters. They would be willing to pay a premium to reduce the variance in their payoff. If they share the costs of providing the engine, they can accomplish this. Let x represent the certainty equivalent dollar value for the lottery that gives the individual's payoff in the absence of the fire engine. We have, $\log (x) = 0.99 \times \log (20\,000) + 0.01 \times \log (10\,000)$. This gives, $x = 19\,861.85$, and $20\,000 - x = 138.15$. To avoid one chance in 100 of a $10 000 loss, each individual in the community would be willing to pay $138.15. This amount can be looked at as the individual's option value for the right to consume at zero cost the fire engine's services at any time during a one-year period. The sum of the individuals' option values would be $13 815, an amount well in excess of the rental price.

While this indicates the nature of the option value it is on efficiency grounds an inferior one to that of the insurance pool system—provided that

(1) there are no institutional constraints against an insurance pool arrangement;

(2) that the administrative costs were not such as to mop up the differential between the cost of the summed option values and the straight insurance pool sum.

What Zeckhauser does not bring out but which is relevant to his example is that while the individuals value their houses in use at

$10 000, there is an additional 'good' which is being bought in the case of the option value analysis of the fire engine. This is the 'good' of the anticipation of the use of the fire engine which may in turn be considered as somewhat akin to the concept of the good of peace of mind. If one knows that a fire engine is available to prevent any fire damage to a house then in the period between taking out this 'option' for the fire engine and the time when a fire might be expected one's level of welfare will be increased to the extent that worry about the damage likely to be incurred should a fire take place is decreased.

A different aspect of option valuation is recognised by Zeckhauser. He claims: 'We have in effect what might be called a utility of variety. Consumers like and get a positive utility from the fact that goods are kept available . . . It is a utility that is defined independently of the use itself. In this way it is quite different from the actuarial aspects of payments for PIP goods (or those that Weisbrod discusses)'.

There are therefore two reasons to believe that option demand will be a real and positive entity. Firstly, there is the demand for the 'good' which is derived from anticipation as opposed to use—the line that Weisbrod tends to advocate; and secondly there is the utility of variety which Zeckhauser opts for. While there is a close link between these two concepts they are separable. While the Zeckhauser concept undoubtedly has merit and validity in indicating the fuller meaning of option demand in a broad framework it does not appear to have much relevance to the concept of option demand in the context of life saving. It is very much the Weisbrod type of approach which is more immediately relevant.

8.2.3 The Perception Problem

Before discussing the relevance of these concepts to life saving, let us consider Zeckhauser's attitude to the vexed question of the misperceptions of individuals in estimating probabilities or risk levels. He poses the following question: 'If individuals calculate their option values on an actuarial basis using consumers' surplus, and if they over-estimate probabilities of use, should we correct this bias?' Zeckhauser suggests in response to this question: 'If all utilities are in use rather than anticipation, we would argue that the community head should modify the stated option values to reflect accurate probability estimates. If utility in anticipation is a meaningful concept, the question is more difficult and will depend on the specific parameters of specific cases'. He continues: 'We would surely agree that the more likely they are to find out, the more desirable it is to correct their misestimates ... The less danger there is of becoming informed, the more blissful is ignorance'.

Within the narrower confines of concern with meeting consumers' satisfactions *ex post* as well as *ex ante*, then there is little with which we might quarrel with Zeckhauser. However, on the question of overall efficiency in allocation and on that of equity as between different groups in the community there is more cause to question Zeckhauser's conclusion. Ignorance may be bliss but why should the allocation of scarce resources in the public sector be allowed to rest on the ignorance of the individual consumer? Why should one group receive less and one group more than their equitable share of the benefits of some public programme solely because one group is better informed than another of the likelihood that various contingencies will or will not occur? As far as utility in use is concerned then it is argued here that where it is possible the objective of any programme ought to be to maximise utility *ex post*. (It is more difficult to be as definite with regard to utility in anticipation but the discussion of this issue will be postponed until chapter 9.) Certainly the normal concern of economists is in determining *ex ante* utilities since it is these which in turn determine the consumers' demand. The fact that consumers 'make mistakes' (in other words, there is a difference between expected utility and realised utility) is normally of little interest to the economist. He will of course be interested to determine the costs which consumers may be prepared to pay to reduce the extent of their ignorance as regards the utility they are likely to realise from a particular purchase. Where the goods in question are by and large publicly provided and the 'community head' or government is in a position to narrow or eliminate the gap between expected and realised utility then it ought to do so. Provided—and it is a major proviso—that consumers are prepared to accept that there are certain areas where 'acting in their own interests' it is better to hand over certain decision-making, or in this particular case knowledge on which to base decision-making to the state (since by so doing they are likely to increase their *ex post* utility), then there is nothing to prevent the state stepping in to correct the misestimates of probabilities by individuals.

8.3 APPLICATION TO VALUATION OF REDUCTION IN RISK

This summary of the concepts of option demand and PIP goods allows us to see the concept of valuation of reduction in risk of death in a somewhat different light. The separation made between 'value in use' and 'value in anticipation' is of particular interest. Although not necessarily the same thing there is a very close association between firstly the concepts of value in use and value in anticipation and secondly those of value of reduction in risk *per se* and value of reduction of anxiety associated with reduced risk respectively.

This approach to the concept used in the previous chapter for valuation of reduction in risk is not different; it merely examines the question from a different angle and thereby aids understanding of the approach. The separation of the two aspects involved makes for a better conceptual framework for the analysis. At the same time it makes the use of the analysis that much more complicated and introduces some difficulties in determining the appropriate life-saving welfare function, an issue considered at some length in chapter 9.

Let us examine the implications of this separation for determining values of reduced risk. One of the criticisms of Jones-Lee's type of approach[4] is that it involves an interviewing procedure to elicit information from individuals as to the values they place on different levels of risk and changes therein. Apart from the general problem of getting individuals to make meaningful responses to hypothetical questions, this separation of the two aspects—risk and associated anxiety—raises doubts as to whether Jones-Lee's type of approach will be able to cope with both of them. It might be argued that individuals can relatively easily make judgments about the values associated with reductions in risk *per se* and it may be right to concur with Schelling[1] that a 1 per cent reduction in risk will be valued the same (*excluding* the anxiety related value) whatever the existing risk level (that is, the value of a change in risk from 10 per cent to 9 per cent valued the same as a change from 5 per cent to 4 per cent). However, we would probably agree with Schelling that the latter of these two points is unlikely to hold good for reduced anxiety or increased peace of mind. And again some doubts must be expressed as to whether the individual in the Jones-Lee 'hypothetical' environment can take full account of the anxiety he might associate with a risk level were he having to face such a risk situation in real life.

There seems no way to resolve this question without some empirical testing of the type of approach adopted by Jones-Lee. If we could accept Schelling's hypothesis on valuation of risk *per se* (as above) then in so far as individuals' responses yielded different values for risk changes from x per cent to $(x - 1)$ per cent than from y per cent to $(y - 1)$ per cent, $y \neq x$, then it could be argued that the individuals were taking some account of valuation of reduced anxiety. Or again if we could establish that individuals were more anxious about one mode of potential death than another when faced with a reduction in risk from x per cent to $(x - 1)$ per cent in both situations and again accepting Schelling's hypothesis, then if individuals valued these changes differently we could argue they would be taking some account of their differing anxiety levels in making their responses. This would be a step forward but only a limited one in that we would have no way of knowing whether in the hypothetical situations facing Jones-Lee's interviewees they were able to take *full* account of anxiety. More important of course is that we have no way at present of knowing whether these hypotheses are right; without these the suggested test breaks down.

One possible way of testing whether individuals in Jones-Lee-style interviews were taking full account of anxiety—and at the same time of testing whether responses to hypothetical questions were an accurate reflection of the individuals' reactions in the real world—would be to compare the values emerging from one or more cases of private behavioural studies (building workers, for example) with those emerging from the use of games theory interviews. If these were similar then we could make the not unreasonable assumption that this situation would hold good in the many more areas where we are interested in valuing life but where no values can be obtained from studying behaviour. If the behavioural values were lower than the Jones-Lee values we would be uncertain whether individuals were not including the anxiety-related values to the full in the Jones-Lee model or whether the values were being distorted by the hypothetical circumstances of the Jones-Lee interview. If they were higher we might argue that only the latter aspect was affecting the values—but we could not be certain that this was more than compensating for an underestimation of the anxiety-related values.

How big a problem this might prove to be is impossible to tell. It does seem right to conceptualise the valuation approach in terms of risk *per se* and associated anxiety or, in the related terms of option values, value in use and value in anticipation. If it transpires that we simply cannot determine the extent to which values emerging from Jones-Lee's approach do take account of anxiety, then we may well have to fall back more than would seem currently desirable on the 'private behavioural' approach or even the 'public behavioural' approach of chapter 6.

REFERENCES

1. Schelling, T. C., The life you save may be your own. In *Problems in Public Expenditure Analysis*, ed. S. B. Chase, Brookings Institute, Washington, 127–162 (1968)
2. Weisbrod, B. A., Collective-consumption services of individual consumption goods, *Q. Jl. Econ.*, August (1964)
3. Zeckhauser, R., Uncertainty and the need for collective action. In *Public Expenditures and Policy Analysis*, eds. R. H. Haveman and J. Margolis, Markham Publishing Company, Chicago (1970)
4. Jones-Lee, M. W., *The Value of Life, an Economic Analysis*, Martin Robertson, London (1976)

9

Decision Rules and the Social Welfare Function for Life-saving Policy Areas

9.1 INTRODUCTION

In an attempt to draw various strands together this chapter examines the decision rules which emerge from the preceding chapters. At the same time this provides an opportunity to summarise some of the main features of the preferred approach to life valuation and set the issues in a policy-orientated framework. In addition the social welfare functions which emerge from the value of risk approach are set out together with the assumptions surrounding them. While this still leaves us some way short of a 'solution' to the questions of demand for life-saving measures and of the appropriate level of investment in mortality-reducing policies, it provides the necessary conceptual background from which it is to be hoped empirical research can eventually draw solutions.

9.2 DECISION RULES

Firstly let us assume no 'externalities' in the sense that the individuals engaged in the appropriate activities are those bearing the risk (for example, drivers faced with the question of wearing seat belts which only affects the risk to themselves).

(1) The valuations placed on the reductions in risk ought to be based on or at the very least reflect the views of the individuals in society.

Here we are concerned with the situation in which (it is assumed) individuals have perfect knowledge of the existing level of risk and the new level of risk after some ameliorative action is taken. We want to answer the question: what value is to be attached to reducing risk from x to $x - y$? We will further assume that all society is equally affected by the change in risk (although the effects on their anxiety levels may differ, one individual to another).

Now we know the value placed by society on a pound of peas, on a loaf of bread and other such marketable commodities through the price/market mechanism. With reductions in risk, were a market available, then the values would similarly be given through the market mechanism. We could establish for a given quantity of output of reductions in risk what the market demand was, that is, what people were prepared to pay. The desirability of the concept of consumer sovereignty is considered as being central to any valuation of life methodology which is to be anything other than imposed.

Part of the problem associated with the human capital approach to valuation of life (see chapter 5 for consideration in detail) is that it makes little if any allowance for consumers' preferences. That approach results in imposed values which at best tell us something about what the minimum values are that society ought to be prepared to pay, but which in practice tell us nothing about what society would be prepared to pay. It is partly for this reason that the valuation of reduction in risk approach has been suggested as preferable. Consequently it is only right to carry it through by insisting that it is the equivalent of market valuations which should determine the values themselves. As Schelling says[1]: 'It is worthwhile to remind ourselves that the people whose lives may be saved should have something to say about the value of the enterprises and that we analysts, however detached, are not immortal ourselves'.

(2) The relevant measurement of the physical level of risk is an objective measurement and not the subjective assessment of individuals.

It is much less straightforward to gain acceptance for this rule or to prove its validity. It is however sufficiently important to justify examining it in some detail. As Schelling[1] puts it: 'John Donne was partly right: the bell tolls for thee, usually, if thou didst send to know for whom it tolls, but most of us get used to the noise and go on about our business'. Fromm[2], however, goes further: 'A man who would risk his life unnecessarily (or throw it away) may be a fool. For a society to take a fool's valuation (either as an explicit or probabilistic expected value) as the correct one is ridiculous'. This appears to go too far. Firstly, although it may be accepted that where public funds are involved we ought not to use a fool's valuation in deciding upon their allocation, if on the one hand society is comprised solely of fools, then the valuation of these fools is the correct one to use. (Who are economists to say that 'they' are fools and we are not?) On the other hand and being more realistic there are undoubtedly differing levels of intelligence among individuals in any society; it seems possible to argue that those with higher intelligence influence the less intelligent and consequently the standard of 'social' decisions is above that which would be obtained from 'representative man' acting in a vacuum (in other words, without influence of his fellow man). Secondly, when is a fool a fool? Who is to decide who is foolish and who is wise? We are all wise and foolish together to differing degrees and in different ways. Thirdly, in our democratic, market-orientated society by and large we do not interfere with individual choice in the market (although we may determine the framework of these markets). The fact that there is a market for striped toothpaste always raises doubts in my mind as to the sanity of my fellow citizens. Equally my zero demand at any price for curry I know raises doubts in some of their minds about mine. I may describe such actions as the purchase of these products as the acts of fools; but I would not legislate against the sale of either product.

No; Fromm goes too far. In so far as he includes the perception of risk in his fool's valuation then together with Schelling I would accept the need to be paternalistic regarding risk perception. The fact that individuals misperceive risk is wholly a function of imperfect knowledge, almost certainly related to the cost of improved knowledge (which may be very great for the individual) and has little if anything to do with attitudes, tastes, or value judgments. (This is not to say that all individuals ought to view risk in the same way.) With perfect knowledge it is possible to say that the level of risk in a given situation is x. The fact that some or all individuals think it is y is irrelevant. With those who would argue that this is an interference with consumer sovereignty, the only reply must be 'well, perhaps'. But it is not suggested that individuals' *values* be overruled nor that in any way the individual is having something imposed on him; merely that when dealing with a situation in which better knowledge is available to the government or the community head than to the individual it is right and proper that the government should use this information with the knowledge that it is better. If it is paternalistic to use the best data available for decision-making even when such data are not available to or not fully comprehended by the general populace, then let us be paternalistic.

However, the question may legitimately be asked: why in this matter and not in the case of striped toothpaste? Abstracting from the question of externalities (which is at least a partial explanation in some cases) the answer is partly a question of degree—the degree of imperfection of knowledge and partly a question of the consequences of error. The man who misperceives the size of his toothpaste tube either gets a shock or a bonus but it is unlikely to be of much consequence to him either way and he will quickly come round to inspecting the size of his toothpaste tube more carefully the next time he makes a purchase. (Even in this area, of course, the government does interfere—particularly in legislating against giant-size detergent packets which are very far short of full.) The man who misperceives the risk of death he faces—and he is much more likely to misperceive this, because of an inbuilt psychological bias—may well suffer much more catastrophically for his error, and may not have the chance to inspect his level of risk a second time around. His misperception is likely to be very much greater because he is not so well informed about his risk of death as he is about the size of his toothpaste. Moreover, while the individual may dismiss a low-level risk of death on the road as being negligible and equate it to zero, the government acting on his behalf and on behalf of the rest of society cannot do so for the simple reason that it has 7000 plus bodies to be counted on the roads each year. Similarly, smokers may discount heavily the risk of lung cancer, but the N.H.S. has to try to ensure that facilities are available to cope with all the services required by lung cancer victims.

In effect the 'imposition' of the objective level of risk is in form like a public good. It is available to all and consumption by one individual does not affect the availability to others. The costs to a single individual to obtain accurate information on the levels of risk he faces in different situations could be enormous. Only the government acting on behalf of society may be in a position to bear these costs. The government could of course stop short of 'imposing' the objective level of risk in decision-making in life-saving activities and simply attempt to inform and educate the public in risk levels. To some extent this is done already. (Recent campaigns to wear seat belts for example have emphasised the risk levels involved in wearing and not wearing seat belts.) However, there are substantial costs involved in this; firstly in the government's providing the information and secondly in the road

128

users taking the trouble to take note and absorb the information. While some might argue that the above is not sufficient to justify the overruling of individual's assessment of risk, a final argument—and one that is not without merit—is that there are areas of decision-making where individuals are prepared to abrogate their consumer sovereignty and let the government act on their behalf. It is argued that the case of assessment of risk levels is one of these areas.

But we cannot press this decision rule too far. While it is argued that the government ought always to try to act in the above manner when concerned with the valuation of risk *per se* this will not necessarily be the case in the valuation of reductions in anxiety associated with changes in risk levels. These anxiety reductions will by definition be based on the perceived risk and consequently there are problems in attempting to operate throughout on the basis of objective risk. Where the perception of risk is inaccurate the anxiety related to this may have to be accepted in some instances as the basis of this part of the decision. In some situations of course it may pay the government to mount a publicity or education programme in an attempt to get individuals to improve their perception and thereby 'move' their anxiety to a more accurate base.

(3) The relevant measurement of the physical change in risk associated with some remedial action is the objective change and not the subjective assessment of the change made by the individuals.

The principles which apply to (2) apply here again. Normally we are not concerned that the individual underperceives or overperceives the change in risk levels, only with what actual change is effected. However, as remarked in the discussion above there will be situations where this rule cannot be applied rigorously.

(4) Due account should be taken of differing levels of anxiety associated with similar risk levels as between individuals or situations.

Just as in the world of investment there are risk-lovers and risk-averters, so it is in the world of fatality risks. The same level of risk faced by two individuals (who are both fully aware of what the level of risk is) may result in one increasing his utility if he is a risk-lover and the other decreasing his utility as a risk-averter. In those areas of activity in which the government may be involved in effecting policy to reduce the risk of mortality, although some classes of individuals (motorcyclists, for example) may be risk-lovers and we possibly all are in some instances, by and large we are probably more concerned with differing degrees of risk-aversion than with risk-loving versus risk-averting. The more averse to risk an individual is, the greater will be his anxiety associated with the risk. Again the same individual faced with equal risks (and knowing them to be equal) in two different circumstances may be more of a risk-averter in one circumstance and have greater anxiety in that circumstance than in the other.

This anxiety is a somewhat peculiar 'economic bad'. As Schelling states[1]: 'It applies equally to those who do not die and to those who do, to people who exaggerate the risk of death as much as if these estimates were true. It counts, and is part of the consumer interest in reducing the risk of death ... What the consumer buys is a state of mind, a picture in his imagination, a sensation'. It is important in particular to note Schelling's point that it applies equally 'to people who exaggerate the risk of death as much as if these estimates were true'. In both the case of individuals who suffer different levels of anxiety about the same known risk-levels and the single individual who suffers different levels of anxiety about the same known risk levels in two different circumstances, it is legitimate in both cases to allow for variations in valuations which result from differing anxiety levels. There is no inconsistency in accepting the variations in anxiety levels and at the same time rejecting (in part) individuals' appraisals of risk levels. Anxiety levels and changes therein are based purely on individuals' feelings and attitudes whereas, as noted above risk can be—and ought to be—measured objectively.

There is, however, a more major point of concern, as has already been touched on in the discussion of decision rules (2) and (3) above. What are we to do about anxiety which is based on a misperception of the level of risk, or again what about the relief of anxiety resulting from a change in the perceived level of risk which is different to the change in actual risk? Despite the possible problems in doing so, the basis of decision-making ought to be as far as is practical a fairly rigid application of the 'objective risk' doctrine. Without doubt anxiety will be based on perceived risk; but in so far as the government is better placed to measure risk and changes therein it ought to try to use these measures as the basis of its decisions. There will none the less be situations when it will have to yield to these values based on misperceptions—but it is important that these be seen as departures from the norm rather than accepted practice.

(5) On grounds of equity even although it may be possible to identify the groups within society affected by a particular remedial action, if that remedial action is financed through public funds then

even if (other than on grounds of differing levels of anxiety associated with the level of risk) the group place a lower or higher valuation on the change than would a representative group of society, the valuation given by the representative group should be used.

This is very obviously an overt value judgment which is subject to the qualification of decision rule (11) (see later, page 134). At first sight it might appear a major rule; in practice it is unlikely to have much effect. This is due largely to the fact that in government policy relating to life saving it is seldom that a specific homogeneous group can be identified as being the sole recipients of the 'reduction in risk' goods. What it is equivalent to—as it stands—is that as regards the provision of publicly financed mortality reductions all persons should be deemed equal except in so far as their levels of anxiety differ from one another when faced with equal risks. It rules out the possibility that those of higher income or wealth who are able to pay more will have reductions of risk for them valued more highly than those of lower income. (This is obviously a working rule which will be dependent on the political climate; if, of course, it was decreed politically that ability to pay and other similar factors ought to be allowed to influence the valuations then this rule could, of course, be altered accordingly.) The question of a consensus emerging for differentiating in the valuations placed on different groups within society is, however, another matter. If society as a whole decrees that some groups—or individuals—the old, the young, the males, the females, the Royal Family, the Cabinet, for example—should be valued differently from the average then this would be quite legitimate.

(6) When an activity is privately financed then no action on the part of the government is required (except possibly to attempt to reduce the extent of imperfection of knowledge or possibly to deem illegal actions which are positively risk-increasing).

In the field of road safety, for example, there are various safety features in which individuals may wish to indulge. Parents can accompany children to school if they so wish; vehicle owners can fit head restraints to their seats, and so on. These are private decisions and individuals can be left to make them as they see fit. There may be cases where simply from a consumer protection point of view individuals should be provided with information by the goverment regarding the potential effects of various purchases or actions. There may even be cases where consumer protection will go so far as to result in a banning of certain features which are positively dangerous—although this is unlikely unless there is a question of external effects which the private decision-maker either ignores or does not take properly into account, for example statuettes on car bonnets were banned because of the injuries they inflicted on other road users—particularly pedestrians. Barring externalities, however, the government ought not to interfere, other than from the more normally accepted form of consumer protection standpoint, in individuals' private decisions regarding risks of mortality—just as it does not in other fields of consumer expenditure. It is not for the government to say that expenditure on head restraints is not justified if such head restraints are privately financed.

(7) Where a publicly financed action is identifiable with a specific group and this group has a different anxiety level associated with the risk involved than would a representative group of society, then due cognisance should be given to this in valuing any reduction in the risk which results in a change in the anxiety level.

Having accepted (see chapter 8) that anxiety levels and changes therein are appropriate components of the life-saving welfare function (subject in most circumstances to these being based on accurate perception), it follows that if two groups of equal size can separately be given risk reductions from an existing equal level to a new equal level for the same public expenditure, then if group A has a greater reduction in anxiety than group B, and both groups' risk perceptions are accurate, then group A should have preference. Anxiety is a real phenomenon and must therefore be taken into account. Once relief from anxiety is accepted in the welfare function, then maximising anxiety relief becomes an acceptable objective (provided normally that the anxiety is 'objectively' based)—even if this results in the spoils going to the very anxious in society.

It follows from this that governments may on occasion have more effect on social welfare as reflected in mortality, by allowing increased weight to be given to the saving of lives in situations which create more than average anxiety for the level of risk involved—even if this means saving fewer lives than could be saved by some other set of measures. This seems some way from the rather crude objectives used in introducing chapter 6; but it is an inevitable consequence of accepting firstly the concept of differential values of life and in addition the concept of anxiety and variations therein into the welfare function.

We now need to introduce 'externalities' more explicitly and this is

132

done in the following decision rules. As an example of what is meant by externalities consider two road safety measures—legislation on seat-belt wearing and on minimum depths for tyre treads. In the first instance the only individuals whose risk will be reduced is the seat-belt wearer. In the second not only are vehicle occupants protected but so also are pedestrians. In the latter instance we can consider the pedestrian as being 'external' in the sense that they are affected by the behaviour and actions of others with regard to care of tyres. Again if I fail to have a smallpox injection I may not only impose 'internal' risks to myself but also create external risks to those with whom I might come in contact.

(8) Where all benefits are external, valuation should be based on the representative group's valuation, or if the external group are identifiable should be adjusted to take account of their different (if it is different) anxiety level. This holds good whether the action giving rise to the benefits is publicly or privately financed.

The introduction of externalities makes the valuation more complex—but what has been said in the earlier decision rules is by and large sufficient to guide us as to what to do about externalities. In this particular case where all benefits are external, the valuation will be based on the representative group's valuation adjusted if possible to allow for the anxiety level of the external beneficiaries. This follows automatically from the decision rule (4). It is perhaps worth emphasising that of course it has nothing to do with the valuations of the 'internal' group. It holds good whether the action is privately financed or publicly financed.

These comments also cover decision rules (9) and (10) below.

(9) Where some benefits are external but not all, and the action is publicly financed, the valuation should be based on the representative group's valuation or if the 'internal' group and the 'external' group are identifiable in terms of differing anxiety levels, the internal group's valuation should be weighted according to their anxiety level and the external group's according to theirs.

(10) Where there is a mixture of external and internal, and the action is privately financed, the 'internal' group's valuation should be quite simply their valuation, the 'external' group's being as in (9) above.

Our final decision rule covers a somewhat separate issue from the valuations discussed under the earlier decision rules and different from giving weight to different levels of anxiety or the valuations of the group under consideration.

(11) Where groups at risk are identifiable in terms of some remedial measure which is publicly financed, society as a whole may wish to place a higher or lower value on such groups than the average.

Here we are concerned with publicly financed projects where society as a whole may want to differentiate in the values placed on different groups within it. For example, children may be deemed to have a higher social value than the elderly, the rich than the poor, and so on. There is no reason—provided society can somehow be persuaded to express its weightings—why such differentiations ought not to be built into the decision rules. But there are great difficulties in obtaining acceptable weights. Taking age for example we might find that lost output by age was a close proxy for the weights to be used—but we have no means of knowing. Lost output or productive potential may be one consideration but others might include replaceability (in the case of children), irreplaceability (in the case of a mother), family responsibilities, lack of caring relatives (the elderly) etc. (see Feldstein[3] for one way of determining relative weights). Despite the difficulties in determining the differentials nonetheless this form of differentiation does appear justified in principle.

At this point it is worth returning to the decision on barriers on motorways (as discussed in chapter 3, section 3.2). The various decision rules listed above would suggest that

(a) almost certainly the risk of cross-over accidents was being exaggerated in the public's mind;

(b) the reduction in risk obtained through erecting barriers was being overstated;

(c) insufficient knowledge was available to the public to gauge the costs and effectiveness of barriers *vis-à-vis* other possible remedial measures; and

(d) the value of the benefits obtained in this particular instance was probably higher than in preventing other accidents of possibly equal severity but in different circumstances.

In what is suggested as an ideal decision-making process as outlined above it would be right and proper that the last of these issues (d) should be the basis of valuation reflecting as it does decision rule (4) above. However the same decision rules would suggest that (a), (b) and (c) should be ignored and supplanted with more factual information, thus basically reflecting decision rules (1), (2) and (3) above. While the information is not available to prove it, nonetheless it is likely that had this 'ideal' decision process been used in this particular instance at least a very similar decision would have been reached.

9.3 THE SOCIAL WELFARE FUNCTION IN DETAIL

9.3.1 *Accurate Perception of Risk*

Having drawn up our decision rules in section 9.2 above, we are now in a position to spell out the life-saving welfare function. The function is somewhat complex. Initially let us assume no externalities, perception wholly accurate, an absolute change in risk always valued the same by the same individual no matter what the circumstances of the existing level of risk and reduction in anxiety directly related to the absolute change in risk. Then the increase in welfare from any reduction in risk of death of α is given by

$$\Delta W_1 = \sum_{i=1}^{i=n} {}_\alpha V_i \qquad (9.1)$$

Where ΔW is the change in welfare, n is the number of individuals whose risk is reduced and ${}_\alpha V_i$ is the value placed by individual i on the reduction α. (In so far as others—i's wife for example—also value the reduction in risk for i then this would be contained in ${}_\alpha V_i$.)

Thus assuming no budget constraint, to achieve the reduction in risk of α for the n individuals, if the cost equals C, then provided that

$$\sum_{i=1}^{i=n} {}_\alpha V_i > C$$

then we have positive net benefits and the measure should be implemented.

Now keeping the assumptions as before but assuming that the existing level of risk influences the values placed by individuals on a change, for any change in the level of risk R, the change in related welfare will be

$$\Delta W_2 = f \left[R, \sum_{i=1}^{i=n} {}_\alpha V_i \right] \qquad (9.2)$$

where R is the existing level of risk and n, i and ${}_\alpha V_i$ are as before.

We thus have a similar situation as in equation (9.1) except that we

135

now assume that as the level of existing risk changes, for a given absolute reduction in risk, so the welfare gain will differ. Again valuation of a change in risk may be dependent on the circumstances surrounding the risk. Then

$$\Delta W_3 = f \left[E, R, \sum_{i=1}^{i=n} {}_\alpha V_i \right] \qquad (9.3)$$

where E is the circumstance surrounding the risk, and the other symbols are as in equation (9.2). ΔW is now dependent on both the existing level of risk and the circumstances surrounding the risk.

Introducing externalities now, if *all* the benefits are external, then we have

$$\Delta W_4 = f \left[E', R', \sum_{j=1}^{j=n'} {}_\beta V'_j \right] \qquad (9.4)$$

where n' is the 'external' population affected; ${}_\beta V'_j$ is the value placed by the 'external' individual j on the reduction in risk β (including any value placed by others on the reduction of β for j); and E' and R' are as before but relate to the 'external' population.

If only part of the benefits are external then

$$\Delta W_5 = f \left[E, R, \sum_{i=1}^{i=n} {}_\alpha V_i + E', R', \sum_{j=1}^{j=n'} {}_\beta V'_j \right] \qquad (9.5)$$

This would normally be the welfare function with which the public sector decision-maker ought to attempt to operate. Since it is assumed that perception is accurate and that anxiety is directly related to the change in risk, there is no need to introduce perceived risk, perceived risk reduction or anxiety directly into this welfare function.

9.3.2 *Misperception of Risk*

If it transpires that perception is not accurate (even after a publicity or education programme) and that the government feels itself compelled to take account of anxiety associated with perceived risk and risk reduction (but not as argued above take account of the value placed

136

on the change *per se* in misperceived risk) the change in welfare can then be written as

$$\Delta W_6 = f\left[E,R, \sum_{i=1}^{i=n} {}_\alpha^r V_i + E',R', \sum_{j=1}^{i=n'} {}_\beta^r V_j' \right.$$

$$\left. + \bar{E},\bar{R}, \sum_{i=1}^{i=n} {}_\alpha^a V_i + \bar{E}',\bar{R}', \sum_{j=1}^{i=n'} {}_\beta^{a'} V_j' \right] \qquad (9.6)$$

where ${}_\alpha^r V_i$ and ${}_\beta^r V_j'$ relate to the valuation of the actual reduction in risk, barred functions relate to the individual's perception and ${}_\alpha^a V_i$ and ${}_\beta^{a'} V_j'$ are the values relating to anxiety (as opposed to reduction in risk *per se*).

We can now continue to make the expression more complex by considering society's views as to the 'relative worth' of different groups in society—the young, the old, the Cabinet, and so on—(see decision rule (11) above). Expression (9.5) above may be taken as the type of welfare function with which the public sector decision-makers will be concerned when remedial action is publicly financed and expression (9.6) above the situation where the government feels it cannot ignore anxiety even if it is based on misperception. In theory at least given these two expressions and knowledge of the likely costs and effectiveness of a publicity programme we could estimate whether the government in particular circumstances ought simply to accept (9.6) or try through publicity to move towards (9.5).

Assuming with no budget constraint that in (9.5) $\Delta W_5 - C$ is negative (that is, the project should not be implemented) and in (9.6) $\Delta W_6 - C$ is positive then if P is known (where P is the cost of a publicity programme to make perception accurate), is $P < C - \Delta W_5$ then it is worth carrying out the education programme. What this means is that if the loss in welfare defined by the difference between C and ΔW_5 (that is, of implementing the project at a loss in terms of the *objectively* defined increase in welfare less the cost of implementation) is greater than the cost of the education programme and *not* introducing the project, then the education programme should be mounted.

Similarly if $\Delta W_5 - C$ is positive, but $\Delta W_6 - C$ negative (that is, the objectively defined benefit is positive but the subjectively defined benefit negative) and the government is prepared *not* to introduce the particular measure, if $\Delta W_5 - C - S > 0$ then the education programme should again be mounted.

The only other case we need consider is that of the privately financed measure, with externalities. In this case ideally we would want those involved in the private financing to take account of the externalities and to do so using the values determined by the 'external' group. In this case we would have

$$\Delta W_7 = f\left[\bar{R},\bar{E}, \sum_{i=1}^{i=n} {}_\alpha V_i + R',E' \sum_{j=1}^{j=n'} {}_\beta V'_j\right] \qquad (9.7)$$

(in other words, the internal group are free to act on their own misperceptions but the 'external' values are determined wholly objectively) or if it were felt that due cognisance had to be taken of the individuals' (external) misperceptions then we would have

$$\Delta W_8 = f\left[\bar{R},\bar{E}, \sum_{i=1}^{i=n} {}_\alpha V_i + R',E', \sum_{j=1}^{j=n} {}_\beta^r V'_j \right.$$

$$\left. + \bar{R},\bar{E}, \sum_{j=1}^{j=n'} {}_\beta^q V'_j\right] \qquad (9.8)$$

There would almost certainly be constraints placed by the government in these circumstances. If, for example, it were the case that if (9.7) were to be defined wholly objectively—as in (9.5) above—then the government would very likely step in to prevent such action, arguing in effect that through their misperceptions the individuals were creating actual harm.

It is also possible that if in (9.7)

$$f\left[R',E' \sum_{j=1}^{j=n'} {}_\beta V'_j\right] < 0$$

or in (9.8)

$$f\left[R',E' \sum_{j=1}^{j=n'} {}_\beta^r V'_j + \bar{R},\bar{E}, \sum_{j=1}^{j=n'} {}_\beta^q V'_j\right] < 0$$

then the government might also step in to prevent action being taken. In these cases the government might in effect argue that even in the event that total welfare was increased if the external benefits objectively defined were negative then it could not permit this to happen. (It would in effect be arguing that the distributional aspects were unacceptable.)

138

9.4 CONCLUSION

While it is of some interest to spell out our decision rules in the detail above and in terms of the changes in the 'life-saving welfare function' it has to be admitted that for some time to come and possibly always, much of the nicety indicated will remain impossible to achieve. The data required—and the cost involved in obtaining the data—may well be such as to make the above sophistication redundant and a much simpler welfare function will be required. The definition of this simpler function will be dependent upon the comparative costs and benefits of introducing the various elements proposed above. Without more empirical research it is not possible to say what form this simpler function would then take.

Nonetheless it is claimed that we have in this chapter the embodiment of the social welfare function as it should be considered in the context of life-saving policy-making. The embracing in this function of firstly the concept of consumer sovereignty (and thence cost-benefit analysis), secondly the value of reduction in risk of death and thirdly the separation of this latter component into risk *per se* and associated anxiety presents a valid conceptual framework within which to seek to improve decision-making in areas involving life saving.

REFERENCES

1. Schelling, T. C., The life you save may be your own. In *Problems in Public Expenditure Analysis*, ed. S. B. Chase, Brookings Institute, Washington, 127–162 (1968)
2. Fromm, G., Comment on Schelling. In *Problems in Public Expenditure Analysis*, ed. S. B. Chase, Brookings Institute, Washington (1968)
3. Feldstein, M. S., Health sector planning in developing countries, *Economica*, May (1970)

Appendix A:
Attitudes to Death

A.1 INTRODUCTION

This appendix represents something of a digression from the main text and a foray into the field of psychology. What it attempts to do is to look behind the questions of behaviour in risk situations, the problems of risk perception, etc. and examine some of the attitudes which individuals and society have towards death and risk of death. It represents a summary of what has been gleaned from a survey of some of the literature in this field of 'psychology of death' and indicates its applicability to this study. While it is unlikely that we will be able to move directly from a study of attitudes to death to valuation nevertheless a knowledge of attitudes may serve to confirm or deny some of the underlying assumptions which we have previously made. At the same time it may provide us with a better understanding of how an experimental framework ought to be devised to allow the value of a reduction in risk approach to be implemented.

While psychology normally plays a relatively small direct role in economics—since economics is primarily concerned with behaviour rather than what motivates behaviour—in this particular field of study in which behaviour may be a poor guide to analysis it is desirable to try to learn what we can from a study of attitudes to death. Consequently in what follows we firstly look at some evidence on attitudes to death, and in particular fear, then consider grief and finally turn to the question of suicide.

A.2 FEAR OF DEATH

'The emotions aroused by death are legion—fear, sorrow, anger, despair, resentment, resignation, defiance, pity, avarice, triumph, helplessness and, to some degree, practically any emotion that there is. The commonest one is fear'[1]. Thus does Hinton introduce his chapter on fear of death and dying. Thereafter he suggests that this fear is necessary for the survival of the race, otherwise we would too frequently put our lives at risk 'unnecessarily'. Hinton maintains that the fear of death is with us in varying degrees from about the age of five onwards. Among young adults it is at a fairly low level whereas among the aged it is present in the majority.

In Swenson's[2] study of attitudes to death among the aged, he found that in a group of 200 individuals over the age of 60, 45 per cent positively looked forward to death and only 10 per cent were prepared to admit to a fear of death. (The rest were 'evasive in their attitudes'.) He also looked at death attitudes according to the circumstances of the individuals concerned and found that the most significant relationship was between individuals engaged in religious activities or having a religious outlook and a forward-looking attitude to death. Individuals living in institutions tended to have a similar attitude, those living with a spouse evaded the issue while those living alone tended to fear death the most. Swenson's main conclusion which is of relevance in this study was that 'fear of death tends to be relatively non-existent in the conscious thought of the aged'.

Whether or not in terms of fear of death religion *is* the opium of the people is far from being proved by Swenson's study but the view is given additional weight in a study by Williamson[3] who echoes the importance of religiosity. He argues that if men believe in an afterlife they will have less cause to fear death. Becker and Bruner[4] take a particularly strong line on this issue and argue that: 'When the belief in immortality is called in question, an almost morbid fear of death arises, or even true thanatophobia'.

Perhaps to summarise this discussion of the relationship between fear of death and religiosity we can again quote from Hinton[1]:

'The belief that eternal life after death is determined by conduct on earth is fading. Individual fantasy of the afterlife appears to hold greater sway than religious teaching. Although this means that during life fewer fear the possibility of eternal hell after death as a deserved punishment for sinful ways, equally the religious belief that this life is a preparation for the next has been diluted almost out of existence. Increasingly few, it seems, are protected from the fear of death by the belief that it is not an annihilation, but the beginning of a fuller life'.

Alexander *et al.*[5] queried the apparent contradiction that whereas one might expect that the great majority of people would show some concern about death, most studies conducted into death attitudes—largely interview and questionnaire studies—up to that time had suggested that most people showed only a very low level of conscious concern over death and that it was only children, old people, and persons in a psychopathological state who showed a higher level of concern. These authors tried to rationalise this by suggesting that in previous studies individuals either had not expressed their true feelings or alternatively had somehow thought that they were not expected to say the things they genuinely felt. In their own study, which was concerned with emotions at a not necessarily conscious level, Alexander *et al.*[5] used a test involving a word association task to measure response time and psychogalvanic response, including certain 'death-associated' words. In the test on a group drawn from Princeton male undergraduates they found that there was a greater emotional response to the death-related words than to neutral words drawn from the general language. By way of explanation for this finding, which tended to contradict the interview and questionnaire studies which had preceded it, Alexander *et al.*[5] suggest that: 'It is likely that we are dealing with two levels of functioning with regard to the death concept. The one involves overt consciously communicated attitudes, the other less conscious processes that can be inferred from response time and P.G.R. measurements'.

On the basis of this the authors argue that concern with death is probably with us at all stages of the life-cycle being more apparent and/or stronger at certain times. They continue

'It may be that at these critical times in the life history man is more conscious of his mortal nature and engages in some serious efforts to provide some solution to the apparent conflict created between his wish to continue life indefinitely and the knowledge that he must eventually die. In less critical times this struggle may be reflected in a constant search for the meaning of life in such things as religious doctrine, philosophy, and science and may determine to some extent the *Weltanschauung* of the individual'.

What we appear to have established so far is that most men fear death (although not necessarily at a conscious level) and fear it throughout their lives. In the life-cycle the fear of death and concern with death tends to ebb and flow, and is for example relatively high among children. There are also observable differences between different groups of people which cannot be explained by the age factor alone. Significant among other factors affecting the degree of fear of death are religiosity and, in the old at least, the nature of their environment, which in turn may be a function of loneliness. As yet we have no evidence that individuals may fear one type of death more than another. However, from observations, from talking with colleagues and friends and from the odd reference to this question in the literature that has been surveyed it would appear that the contention that fear of death may vary with the nature of death is most likely to be correct. Certainly the level of fear is affected by whether the death is outright and painless or slow and full of suffering. For example Hinton reports: 'If dying is thought of as suffering, then it undoubtedly arouses fear; when people have been asked how they wish to die, the almost universal hope has been for a swift, peaceful exit from life'. Cappon found[6] that: 'an overwhelming number of people, 80 per cent to 95 per cent ... say that they want to die suddenly; and appear to want this at all costs'. He suggests that 'this probably represents the strength and universality of the fear of actually dying—as opposed to awareness, acceptance of the notions of death'.

This is, however, to introduce a distinct difference between deaths, that is, the presence or absence of pain. Given the terrible choice between death from starvation and death by hanging who would not choose hanging? What would be of further value, however, would be evidence to support the contention that even deaths which may be considered as more or less immediate and painless are not necessarily feared equally—assuming an equality in the level of risk involved, for example is it immaterial to the victim if he is executed by hanging rather than by the guillotine or in the electric chair?

A further area in which no answers have been obtained and where knowledge would be useful to our approach to life valuation is with regard to the setting in which death or risk of death is encountered. Do we, for example, fear death from fire more in our own homes than at the theatre; or is it that if there is a difference it stems not so much from differences in the level of fear but more in terms of differences in the standards of safety which we expect in different areas of our lives? This latter point may in part be a matter of experience; we have come to expect that travelling by train is a 'safe' way to travel whereas travelling by car we accept a much lower level of safety. We require more empirical data before we can reach any very firm conclusions on this particular issue.

A.3   GRIEF

Before turning to the question of those who voluntarily take their own lives—the suicide case—it is worth dealing briefly with the issue of grief. Various studies report on the effects and consequences of grief and bereavement. Of particular interest in the context of attitudes to death and also on the question of interdependencies of utilities between lives is the effect of a death on the mortality rate of the close survivors. A study by Young et al.[7] of 4486 widowers over the age of 54 found that their death rate in the six months immediately following bereavement was increased by nearly 40 per cent. Thereafter the mortality rate quickly returned to around the level for married men of the same age. Rees and Lutkins[8] tended to confirm these findings, indicating that in their study 4.8 per cent of close relatives of persons who died in the period 1960–65 died within one year of bereavement compared with only 0.7 per cent of a comparable control group of non-bereaved people. The figure for widows and widowers was particularly high—12 per cent. While the diseases which cause these deaths are many the most frequent cause would appear to be heart disease. Thus 'dying from a broken heart' may be a not inaccurate description of at least some of these deaths which occur in the early stages of bereavement. Apart from this increased mortality rate among the bereaved, the emotions accompanying bereavement may include grief, shame, guilt—sometimes even a sense of relief. Frequently a period of mental illness or of depression may follow the death of a close person. Parkes[9] has studied the relationship between bereavement and mental illness. He writes: 'I compared the number of spouse bereavements which had actually occurred in the psychiatric population with the number that could have been expected to occur by chance association ... It transpired that 30 of the 94 patients had been admitted for illnesses which had come on within six months of the death of a spouse, whereas only five spouse-bereaved patients would have been expected by chance alone'. Hinton[1] reports that: 'Continued incapacitating grief is the commonest variation of the usual pattern of mourning ...'.

144

Cartwright *et al.*[10] report that in their study 'there was some slight evidence that the more severely restricted the person who died had been and the longer the period of restriction before death the less likely were their relatives to seek medical care because of their bereavement'. This same study indicated a difference between the sexes as to the extent of medical attention required in bereavement. 'Seven out of ten (widows) had consulted their doctor since their bereavement compared with three-fifths of the widowers, half of them had done so in connection with their bereavement, compared with one-third of the widowers. Over a third of them had been visited at home by their doctor compared with a sixth of the widowers'. One of the more unexpected findings of this study was that 'the proportion of respondents who had consulted a doctor since their bereavement decreased with their age, from 59 per cent of those under 65 to 45 per cent of those 75 or over'. In this study general practitioners were asked about the medical care of the close bereaved. Over half thought that close bereaved should not be given some medical or nursing supervision, about a third that they should receive some medical supervision and about 8 per cent that they should have nursing supervision.

Sufficient has now been stated to indicate that the effects of bereavement can be very real and in some cases very long lasting. While one cannot agree with the way in which Dawson[11] has attempted to solve the problem of valuation of grief, there can be little doubt after what has been said that he is absolutely right to attempt to include it in his calculations. For us, in considering the value of a reduction in risk approach the above comments serve to indicate the need to take some account of interdependencies between lives. This is particularly so where the victims are very young and the grief of parents can be both acute and chronic (particularly if the parents consider themselves to be at fault in any way). In circumstances where death is sudden and unexpected then again the grief will be great since the bereaved will have had no time to prepare themselves for the death and are consequently likely to be more severely stricken.

A.4   SUICIDE

It has been assumed throughout this work that there is positive utility to be obtained from living. It is inherent in all that has been said that man is prepared to make sacrifices to avoid positive risks of death;

145

and further, that this allows a framework to be developed within which some attempt can be made to place a value on this risk avoidance and ultimately on life itself. This positive utility can be viewed in two separate ways or as a combination of these two ways. Man may have a neutral attitude to death itself but value extending life. At the other extreme, man may have a neutral attitude to life, but fear death in such a way that his apparent desire to extend his life may be wholly a function of his disutility associated with the act of death *per se*. Again, man's wish to extend life may be a function of both a wish to live and a wish to avoid death.

In the normal course of events such statements are unexceptional; but what of those cases where individuals decide to terminate their own lives? How does suicide fit into our scheme of things? Why, in what is such a personal act—presumably the most personal act an individual can commit—is it possible to indicate 'trends' in a society's suicide rate?

Now if we set 'life' in terms of an economic good and 'living' in terms of the cost of having the economic good, we might say that for the individual who kills himself the costs of living outweigh the benefits of life or in possibly more acceptable terms, the disutility associated with continued living is so great as to more than counterbalance the utility of being alive.

It is important to note here that we are dealing very much with the views of individuals. It might easily be postulated that the individual who contemplates suicide may be overplaying his current misfortune, or overreacting to some particularly disastrous situation. Were he to consider the matter rationally or discuss it with others, then this might affect his assessment of the situation. Again, although suicide is by definition a personal act, it can frequently involve relationships with others. It is certainly not unknown for suicide—or attempted suicide—to be used to hurt others. On the other hand, the awareness that suicide can hurt others may sometimes act as a deterrent on would-be suicides. Of course the death act itself may have certain costs associated with it. There is a social stigma attached to suicide and in some religions it is considered a sin. Predominantly Roman Catholic countries such as Italy, Spain and Ireland tend to have comparatively low suicide rates and it was only in 1961 that the statute against attempted suicide in England was abolished. Even if these factors do not deter the would-be suicide, the actual physical act of killing oneself, the fear of death itself (as opposed to simply 'halting' life) may do so.

146

Who commits suicide? Can such persons be dismissed as 'freaks' or as in some way atypical? May[12] writes that 'epidemiological studies have indicated that the aged, the mentally ill, those dependent on alcohol and other drugs, migrants and persons from socially disorganised areas, the socially isolated and those who come from broken homes, are all exposed to higher risk of suicide'. May's description of the higher risk groups suggests that those more prone to suicide and attempted suicide are for various reasons not leading what might be termed normal existences.

Most societies tend to condemn suicide and also to some extent fear suicide as striking at the whole edifice on which society rests. To 'opt out' of society by committing suicide is at the same time to say that there is 'something rotten in the state of Denmark' and leaves society with a bad taste in its collective mouth. It is perhaps not surprising that society attempts to rid itself of the bad taste by branding suicides as being of disturbed mind and not the acts of rational, mature minds. Suicide is thus designated deviant behaviour—thereby reducing the element of potential threat to society. Is there medical evidence to support this? Certainly May includes 'the mentally ill' and 'those dependent on drugs and alcohol' as being among the high-risk groups but in his terms at least these two groups do not explain the whole population of suicides. Hanlon[13] quotes a study by Robins et al.[14] who found that '98 per cent of the suicides they studied had been clinically ill and 94 per cent of them psychiatrically ill. Of the group, 68 per cent had been suffering from one of two diseases: manic-depressive depression or chronic alcoholism'. Hanlon concludes that 'careful studies have shown that the most significant characteristic of those who attempt suicide is that they are in a state of frank psychosis'. May[12] confirms Hanlon's psychological/sociological perspective.

'Suicide is not a simple variable that can be correlated directly with another single feature of society. Social isolation, social attitudes, feelings of belonging, self-valuation according to social norms; all these are important but cannot tell the whole story. Purely sociological explanations ignore the intra-personal struggles that these environmental situations produce, and in the same way purely psychological interpretations fall short of a comprehensive explanation'.

What does come over very strongly from the study of suicide is that it is very much more of a sociological phenomenon than one might think in view of the apparently very personal nature of the suicide act. But within this it is the individual or personal situation which determines who the suicides will be. It would seem that those who commit suicide are likely to be mentally ill and society's designating them 'of unsound mind' is more than just an attempt by society to retain an easy conscience. Given this, suicide ceases to be of particular relevance to our study. We do not have to find a detailed rationale within our model to explain the case of suicide; we can simply dismiss it as a psychological phenomenon outside of normal behaviour. We can therefore defend our basic assumption—that rational man is prepared to make some sacrifice (pay some cost) to continue his existence. This conclusion is subject to qualification in that there may be a (presumably small) section of the community at the margin who, although not obtaining any positive utility from living, do not commit suicide because of the costs associated with such an act and/or of the awareness of the costs which would fall on relatives and friends.

REFERENCES

1. Hinton, J., *Dying*, Penguin Books, Harmondsworth (1967)
2. Swenson, W. M., Attitudes toward death among the aged, *Minn. Med.*, 42 (1959)
3. Williamson, P., Fear in elderly people, *J. Amer. Geriatr. Soc.*, **1**, 739–742 (1953)
4. Becker, H., and Bruner, D., Attitude toward death and the dead and some possible causes of ghost fear, *Ment. Hyg.*, **15**, 828–837
5. Alexander, I. E., Colley, R. S., and Alderstein, A. M., Is death a matter of indifference? *J. Psychol.*, 43 (1957)
6. Cappon, D., Attitudes of and towards the dying, *Can. Med. Ass. J.*, **87**, 693 (1962)
7. Young, M., Benjamin, B., and Wallis, C., The mortality of widowers, *Lancet*, 2 (1963)
8. Rees, W. D., and Lutkins, S. G., Mortality of bereavement, *Br. Med. J.*, **4**, 13 (1967)
9. Parkes, C. M., *Studies of Grief in Adult Life*, Tavistock Publications, London (1972)
10. Cartwright, A., Hockey, L., and Anderson, J. L., *Life Before Death*, Routledge and Kegan Paul, London (1973)

11. Dawson, R. F. F., *Cost of Road Accidents in Great Britain*, Road Research Laboratory (1967)
12. May, A. R., Suicide—a world health problem. In *Suicide and Attempted Suicide, Skandia International Symposia*, eds. J. Waldenström, T. Larsson and N. Ljungstedt, Stockholm (1972)
13. Hanlon, J. J., *Principles of Public Health Administration*, C. V. Mosby, St. Louis, chapter 23, 5th edn. (1969)
14. Robins, E., Murphy, G. E., Wilkinson, R. H., Gassner, S., and Kayes, J., Some clinical considerations in the prevention of suicide based on a study of 134 successful suicides, *Am. J. Public Hlth.*, July (1959)

Appendix B:
Discounting—The Valuation of Life-saving Benefits Through Time

B.1 THE NATURE OF DISCOUNTING

B.1.1 *Introduction*

One of the problems faced in estimating the benefits of any life-saving measure or policy is that the benefits normally will not accrue at the one point in time but will be spread over a number of years. For example, the building of a coronary care unit may be assumed to reduce deaths from heart disease not only in the first year of its operation but over future years as well. Even if we have an acceptable method for evaluating the benefits in the first year, how would we extend this to the valuation of benefits arising in the future?

The normal way to handle this type of situation is through discounting, which allows a future stream of benefits or costs to be equated with a certain sum now (the 'present value'). The literature on the theory and practice of discounting is extensive and the reader who wishes to pursue the concept more fully will find a number of references at the end of this appendix. However, it may be useful to indicate briefly what the general concept of discounting is about. Let us assume that the cash from a particular investment is the same in each year over the next 20 years and then ceases. The only cost involved is the initial cost of the scheme, in other words there are no running or maintenance costs and the scrap value of the equipment is zero at the end of the 20 years. Now if the initial cost is £20 000 and the annual benefits in each of the next 20 years are £1010 then it might be argued that we should proceed with this investment because the sum of the benefits (£20 200) exceeds the sum of the costs (£20 000). But it is far from certain that this is a correct conclusion.

150

For example if the original £20 000 were to be banked and interest accumulated then after 20 years the amount including interest altogether would be considerably in excess of £20 000, and unless the rate of interest paid by the bank was extremely small, considerably in excess of £20 200. Again it is unlikely that an individual would be prepared to lend the reader a sum of £20 000 now and be content with his returning the same sum in one year's time, even if the inflation rate were zero.

Feldstein[1] defines the discount rate calculation as 'a functional relationship that makes outputs at different points in time commensurable with each other by assigning to them equivalent present values'. From this it follows that the present value of the costs of one project can be compared with the present value of the benefits of that project and the 'net present value' calculated, that is, the difference between the discounted stream of costs. Given a straight choice as to whether or not to proceed with a project if the net present value is non-negative then the decision should be to proceed. Where a number of projects are being considered the use of the discounting calculations will allow the net present value of project A to be compared with the net present value of project B with that of project C and so on.

B.1.2 *Why Should the Rate be Positive?*

But why should we assume that the discount rate will be positive? Henderson[2] indicates three reasons why this should be so. Firstly, 'expected future consumption is subject to risk and uncertainty', secondly it is 'rationally implied by the inevitability of death'; and thirdly, as the level of real consumption per head of a community increases, each absolute addition to it will yield successively smaller increases in economic welfare, that is, the marginal utility of consumption decreases through time. In addition there is a fourth reason, one which is mentioned explicitly by Dasgupta and Pearce[3]: 'Society simply does prefer the present to the future—there is "pure myopia"'.

Henderson's second point—that a positive rate is rationally implied by the inevitability of death—is particularly interesting in our present study because any successful investment in life saving will by definition reduce the mortality rate and thereby (following Henderson) reduce the discount rate. Henderson writes 'If I have an assurance of £100 in 20 years time, it is not rational of me to regard this as equivalent to £100 now, since although it is certain that I shall receive the money if I survive, it is not certain that I shall survive'. To determine the present value of the £100 it would need to be multiplied by the probability of its being received which is equivalent to discounting at a positive rate. Henderson estimates that for a country like Britain this mortality factor on its own is likely to suggest a discount rate of about 1 per cent. Whatever the actual size of the mortality factor we can say with certainty that it will always be positive. (To obtain a negative rate of discounting from the mortality factor would require something greater than a 100 per cent probability of survival over some future period of time, which is clearly a nonsense.)

All the above points are based on the concept of social time preference which has been defined by Feldstein[1] as follows: 'A social time preference function assigns current values to future consumptions: it is a normative function reflecting society's evaluation of the relative desirability of consumption at different points in time'. All are in some way or other associated with the concept of the choice between present and future consumption. But there is another way of considering what the appropriate rate is for application in public investment appraised. This is the 'social opportunity cost' rate, which has been defined, again by Feldstein[1] as 'a measure of the value to society of the next best alternative use to which funds employed in the public project might otherwise have been put'.

We can see that, given the normal set of circumstances in which the return to investment is positive, in arriving at the social opportunity cost rate, the 'next best alternative use' to which the funds we are concerned with might be put will normally yield a positive rate of return. Consequently, given the rationale of the social opportunity cost rate we have here yet another reason for expecting the rate of discount to be positive. We need not concern ourselves with the problems associated with determining the actual magnitude of the discount rate. What we can say is that the use of discounting techniques (at some reasonable positive rate of interest) and the type of framework which such use requires for decision-making is to be recommended in the public sector. This is sufficient for our present purposes.

152

B.2 THE APPLICATION OF DISCOUNTING TO LIVES SAVED

B.2.1 *Some Difficulties*

Moving to the more specific problem with which we are currently faced, ought we to use discounting techniques in valuing the benefits of lives saved through time? If so what is the rationale behind doing so? And can we determine the appropriate rate of interest to use?

Let us consider what is entailed in discounting in the area of life saving. Is it the case that the present value of a life saved in ten years time is less than the value of a life saved today? Is the social opportunity cost rate and/or the social time preference rate as they are normally used applicable in the case of lives saved? Obviously *an individual* would prefer to be saved from death today rather than saved from death in ten years time. However, given the nature of the problem this is not the choice that exists. More precisely the question we want to answer is of the following nature. Given two families A and B, both of which are identical but for the fact that all members of family B are ten years older than their counterparts in family A, should we place a higher value on preventing the death of the oldest son in family B today than on preventing the death of the oldest son in family A in ten years time?

Now ignoring for the present the question of risk and uncertainty we must consider whether in this context a positive rate of discounting is as Henderson suggests[2] 'rationally implied by the inevitability of death'. Now if this applies (and it can be readily argued that it does because in the intervening ten years in our example the oldest son in family A could die anyway) then we have one reason for applying a positive discount rate, although it is likely to be small. Marglin[4] questions whether in fact all the mortality effect, small as it may be, should be used. He states: 'The brevity and uncertainty of life may influence an individual's disposition of his income in favour of the present, but—since the generations yet to be born are every bit as important as the present generation—the present generation's preference should not be allowed full sway in determining the overall rate of investment'. This is Marglin's 'authoritarian answer' which he claims is very similar to Pigou's[5] ideas in *The Economics of Welfare*. We can argue, however, that the weight given to future generations is a normative political decision. Hence in the *social* time-preference function this weight is likely to be greater than that given by private individuals and hence in the private time-preference function. Since Henderson's 1 per cent is suggested for the private-preference function, this implies that in the social time-preference function we are dealing with a discount rate (which is 'mortality induced' so to speak) of something less than 1 per cent, and depending upon the views of the government, it could be zero in the limit.

The other reason advanced by Henderson for applying a positive discount rate—diminishing marginal utility through time as consumption rises—is difficult to apply in the case of lives saved. In the accounting type of approach to valuation the methodology is based on the benefits derived by an individual (to a lesser extent by his family, and to a still lesser extent by the rest of society) from not dying. Now in the case of a fatality it is literally all or nothing and it is difficult to see how, in adopting this approach, we can use a marginal utility approach. It is also difficult to establish—if indeed it is possible at all—the relationship between on the one hand lives saved, limbs broken, and utility and on the other increasing consumption through time. An extra few pounds of consumption in ten years time is such a completely different concept from that of being saved from death in ten years time (and all that this implies) that the normal logic of discounting appears to break down.

Feldstein encounters this difficulty. He states[1]: 'Aggregation over time raises difficult problems. A stream of dollar increments to national consumption can be aggregated by calculating the present value when discounted at a social time–preference rate. The basic justification for dicounting future increments to consumption is that the marginal utility of consumption falls as *per capita* consumption rises. This reasoning provides no justification for discounting future non-dollar benefits such as lives saved. If a life saved next year is of equal value with a life saved now, the appropriate aggregate is the total number of lives saved'. Feldstein claims[1] that the weights given to the different elements of health benefits (discounted future earnings, reduced numbers of deaths in different age groups, reduced permanent impairments, and reduced short-term disabilities) 'must ultimately reflect the value judgments of the politically responsible officials' and thus that the weights given to mortality must reflect the social value of 'life and not of the livelihood'. He thus suggests that the normal process of discounting does not apply and that if we are to value lives saved in future years at some value different from that of lives saved

154

today then economics has nothing to say on the subject. He implies that the relative values to be placed on lives saved at different times is a political matter based on a political answer (and not an economic one) to the question: What is the relative value of a life saved in ten years time compared to the value of a life saved today?

Broussalian suggests that discounting is meaningless in the case of non-marketable benefit streams. He states[6]: 'Each benefit stream represents an opportunity to consume that, and only that, profile of benefits. Its present value were it to be computed, would not represent a potential for consuming alternative benefit streams (involving intertemporal redistribution) since it is not possible to utilise market or exchange opportunities outside the two production processes'. Broussalian in effect maintains that discounting as such is in these circumstances not valid.

However, the decision-maker will have to make some sort of intertemporal comparison. Broussalian is discussing defence projects but the argument appears completely analogous to life-saving projects and implies that discounting future lives saved is meaningless. While it may be that the decision-maker prefers to have a life saved today rather than another life a year hence, such a valuation must be based on the decision-maker's subjective judgment (influenced certainly by the views of society) and not on economic theory.

Mishan has examined the same concept. He writes[7]:

'The stream of primary benefits [which he defines as "those which would exist in the absence of all opportunities for reinvestment"] attributable to a public investment may exceed the stream of primary revenues that are actually collected ... if a part or all of any benefit does not accrue as cash receipts during the period in question, then that part, or all, of the benefit is not available for reinvestment, and may therefore be regarded as consumption which is constrained to take place within the period. It follows that the policy-maker may choose an investment project, A, having a somewhat smaller primary return within each period than an alternative project, B, simply because the reinvestment potential of the latter is known to be restricted'.

It is immediately obvious that the problems associated with the concept of reinvestibility apply to the analysis of some of the benefits from projects involving life saving and certainly to the problem of the

155

intertemporal comparison of lives saved. The problem of rein-vestibility is certainly not peculiar to such benefits as lives saved. A large proportion of benefits in areas involving life saving are non-revenue, non-reinvestible and to that extent the question of what to do about the problem of non-reinvestibility looms large. Despite this the problem of non-reinvestibility is basically a problem for cost-benefit analysis as a whole and since any solution devised to meet this problem would be an across-the-board solution, the reinvestibility question is not analysed further here.

In the human capital approach we face certain difficulties regarding the valuation of future benefits. The normal logic of discounting does not appear to be applicable. Discounting theory is based on a marginal analysis and the accounting approach is not. For the valuation of life-saving benefits on an intertemporal basis, since economics—positive economics that is—seems unable to be of assistance, if the accounting approach is to be adopted we would (à la Feldstein and Broussalian) have to rely on a decision-maker's subjective judgment as to the weights to be given to life-saving benefits at different points in time. This is far from satisfactory in that the decision-maker may not be able to make such a judgment, or may make it badly or inconsistently. What the analysis above has indicated is that having already mounted a fairly hostile attack on the human capital approach in chapter 5, in considering the problems of discounting as related to the accounting approach, we find further fuel to feed the flames of discontent with that methodology. When we turn to the 'reduction in risk' approach some of the difficulties we have encountered in applying discounting to the human capital approach disappear or at least diminish.

B.2.2 *The Removal of Some of the Difficulties*

In the 'reduction in risk' approach our base point is the determination of how much individuals are prepared to pay out of present income or wealth to reduce the risk of death. Given a fixed reduction in risk, k, we assume that the individual adjusts his income (and/or consumption or wealth) to maximise his expected utility, where utility is a function of income (and/or consumption or wealth), leisure (if this is not constant) and the risk of death. At the margin it is assumed that he will trade-off one pound of income (wealth and/or consumption of other goods) to purchase some reduction in mortality.

We thus have a marginal analysis in which increased safety is a good like any other good except that the price of the good in this case is taken as the amount the individual is prepared to pay for the good rather than the price determined by market forces. But the really important aspect as regards discounting is that with the reduction in risk approach we can operate at the margin. (It was largely because this did not hold good for the 'accounting' approach that led to most of the difficulties we encountered there.) Given this we are now in a position to apply Feldstein's[1] statement of the justification for discounting—'the marginal utility of consumption falls as *per capita* consumption rises'. We have moved away from the concept of all or nothing, living or dying and have introduced, by way of probability theory, a continuous function with all possible values between the certainty of death (probability of unity) and certainty of life (probability of zero). If it proves possible to obtain individuals' revealed preferences for probabilities of living (and, of course, dying) then we can use the marginal analysis and we can use Feldstein's *raison d'être* for the use of a positive discount rate. The other reasons for discounting at a positive rate also hold good with the exception of Broussalian's objection, in other words, we are still dealing with non-marketable benefit streams. It is only in a relatively few cases that 'reduction in risk' benefits are marketable. However, by moving to the reduction in risk approach we are much closer to a situation in which the benefits *could* be marketable. Despite what Broussalian says it is contended that all that is required for discounting to apply is not the goods or benefits in question are marketable; rather that they *could be* marketable. While this does not hold for the 'goods' of lives saved under the accounting approach it does hold for the reduction in risk approach. This is sufficient to overrule Broussalian's objection to discounting or rather the normal rules of discounting.

B.3 CONCLUSION

What the above analysis has indicated is that whereas with the 'accounting' approach to valuation of life we get into all sorts of difficulties when faced with the intertemporal comparison of benefits and therefore the question of discounting, when we move to the 'reduction in risk' approach these difficulties while they do not necessarily disappear at least become more manageable within the normal rules of discounting. Broadly this discussion of discounting

157

has indicated that aside from all the other advantages of using the value of a reduction in risk approach when we come to the practical problem of summing the value of lives saved over a period of years we are in a much better position to cope. We have here yet another reason for preferring the 'reduction in risk' approach.

REFERENCES

1. Feldstein, M. S., The social time preference discount rate in cost-benefit analysis, *Econ. J.*, June (1964)
2. Henderson, P. D., Notes on public investment criteria in the United Kingdom, *Bull. Oxford Univ. Inst. Econ. Stat.*, Feb. (1965)
3. Dasgupta, A. K., and Pearce, D. W., *Cost-Benefit Analysis: Theory and Practice*, Macmillan, London, 137 (1972)
4. Marglin, S. A., The social rate of discount and the optimal rate of investment, *Q. J. Econ.*, Feb. (1963)
5. Pigou, A. C., *The Economics of Welfare*, London (1932)
6. Broussalian, V. L., *The Evaluation of Non-Marketable Investments*, The Franklin Institute, Washington D.C., Oct. (1966)
7. Mishan, E. J., Normalisation procedure for public investment criteria, *Econ. J.*, Dec. (1967)

Appendix C: Some Values of Life

Source	Value of life	Comments
Screening of pregnant women to prevent stillbirths[1]	£50	If screening of maternal oestriol excretion takes place, estimated that the cost per stillbirth averted would be £50. Claimed not widely used at the time. Consequently £50 maximum value
Government decision not to introduce childproof containers for drugs[2]	£1000	Government refused to introduce childproof containers for drugs on grounds of expense. Estimates made that such containers could save 20 to 30 children's lives each year. At the same time they would reduce cost of treating the 16 000 children admitted to hospital each year because of a lack of childproof containers. Saving of approximately £480 000 per annum. Cost of childproofing estimated at £500 000 per annum. Therefore net cost of £20 000 per annum required for saving of 20 children's lives. Since Government didn't proceed, it was claimed that child's life implied to be worth less than £1000
Motorway driving behaviour[3]	£94 000	If optimum motorway speed is assumed equal to the average of 58.8 mph, petrol is assumed to cost 35p per gallon (the price at the time the article was written) and the value of time is taken as £1.00 per hour then the implied value of life can be estimated to be £94 000. To arrive at life as opposed to average casualty weights were derived from Dawson's values
Legislation on tractor cabs[4]	£100 000	At a total cost of £20 million for fitting tractors with cabs, estimated that 200 lives would be saved—implying minimum value of life of £100 000

US defence expenditures and pilot compensation for risky flying[5]	$200 000	Estimated from risk premiums demanded by about 900 individuals for risky jobs
Proposals for improved safety of trawlers[6]	£1 million	Proposals for improved safety of trawlers. Estimate that cost per death averted would be about £1 million
Change in building regulations following collapse of Ronan Point highrise flats[6]	£20 million	From the report of enquiry following the collapse of Ronan Point, a highrise block of flats in London, Sinclair and his colleagues estimated (i) the risk of a gas explosion causing a progressive collapse of such highrise flats; (ii) the cost of raising the safety standards of such existing buildings and the additional cost of constructing new buildings to the higher standards; and (iii) the resultant fall in the risk of such occurrences. From these figures they showed that the implied value of life was in excess of £20 million
Court Award, Pell versus Metropolitan Police and others[7]	£21 500	Policeman, aged 39, would have been earning about £2500 per annum at time of trial. Would have remained in police for at least another five years. Widow aged 40, daughter 14, and son 11. Gave wife £15 to £20 per week for housekeeping. Family's dependency assessed at £28 to £30 per week. Total awarded: £21 500 (of which £750 to daughter and £1250 to son)
Court Award, Thorpe and Easey versus Waspe and Elford	£6300	Lorry driver aged 59. Would probably have worked beyond 65. Widow aged 54 at date of accident. No children. Dependency agreed on £15 per week. Funeral expenses £40.87 (after one-third reduction for contributory negligence). Fatal Accident Award £4200 after one-third reduction for contributory negligence. Implied value of life therefore $£4200 \times \frac{3}{2}$, which equals £6300
Department of the Environment[8]	£39 300	Based on Dawson approach, 1976 prices

Source	Value of life* £	Deceased	Relative
Solatium Awards in Scottish courts[9]	2250 800	Male aged 53	(Widow, son aged 16)
	750 each	Male aged 21	Parents
	250 each	Female aged 10	Parents
	4000 150 each	Male aged 63	(Widow, three married sons living away from home,
	300		son aged 17 at home)
	2000	Male	Widow aged 49
	900	Male aged 10	Parent
	650 each	Male aged 17	Parents

* These figures cover *only* the 'non-financial' value

References
1. Heys, R. F. Oakey, R. E., Scott, J. S. and Stitch, S. R. Practicability and cost of oestriol assays for saving babies in a maternity hospital, *Lancet*, 331–332, Feb. 17th (1968)
2. Gould, D., A groundling's notebook, *New Sci. Sci. J.*, July 22nd (1971)
3. Ghosh, D., Lees, D. and Seal, W., Optimal motorway speed and some valuations of time and life, *Manchester School Econ. Soc. Stud.*, **43**, No. 2, 134–143, June (1975)
4. Sinclair, T. C., Costing the hazards of technology, *New Sci.*, October 16th (1969)
5. Carlson, J. W., *Valuation of Life Saving*, unpublished doctoral dissertation, Harvard University (1963)
6. Sinclair, T. C., Marstrand, P. and Newick, P., Human life and safety in relation to technical change, *Science Policy Research Unit, University of Sussex*, April (1972)
7. Kemp, D. A. M., *The Quantum of Damages*, Sweet and Maxwell, London, 4th edn. (1975)
8. *Department of the Environment Memorandum*, London, HMSO (1976)
9. *J. Law Soc. Scot.*, February to July (1976)

Index

Drèze, 89, 98
Driving behaviour and life values, 108, 159
Driving speed and life values, 107
Dublin and Lotka, 54

Equity, in decision rules, 130
Euthanasia, 20
Externalities, 21
  in decision rules, 132

Feldstein, 134, 151, 152, 154, 157
Fire engines, valuation of, 119–120
Fromm, 126

Ghosh *et al.*, 108
Gloag and Henderson, 85
Grief, 144–145
Grossman, 42

Hanlon, 147
  approach to life valuation, 64–69
Harris, 83
Harris and Hartz, 85
Harrison, 6, 10, 72
Health care
  application of cost benefit analysis, 36–38
  demand, 42–44
  implied values, 79–80
  whose values?, 42–45
Health indicators, 46–48
Heart transplant, implied value of, 79
Henderson, 151, 153
Hine, 79
Hinton, 140, 141, 144
Hirshleifer, 91
Housewives' lives, 56
Housewives' services, 61
Human capital
  and education, 52
  and valuation of life, 54–56
  case studies in life values, 58–69
  definition of, 50–51
  values gross of consumption, 56
  values net of consumption, 56

Implied values, 71
  in health care, 79–80
Intangibles, 15
Interdependencies, between lives, 144
Ison, 85

Jones-Lee, 9, 97
  approach of, 122
  methodology of, 102
  questionnaire of, 109–110
  theoretical contribution of, 91–93
Journal of the Law Society of Scotland, 85

Kidney, machines, 75
  cost–benefit analysis of, 3
Kidney transplants
  implied concern in, 111
  implied values in, 80
Klarman, 44, 54
  approach to life valuation of, 63–64
Klarman *et al.*, 3
Kletz, 105

Life insurance, 106–107
Lifelong support, 82–83
Lone yachtsman, 80–82
Lung cancer, implied values of, 79

Marglin, 153
May, 147
Melinek, 107
Mill, 21
Mishan, 82, 155
  contribution to valuation of life of, 93–96
Motorway barriers, 30–34

N.E.D.C., 104
Needleman, 110
von Neumann and Morgenstern, 91
Newton, 15, 16

Objective risk, 11, 126, 128

164